SRI AUROBINDO
AND
THE CRIPPS MISSION

Sri Aurobindo and The Cripps Mission

Edited by
Sunayana Panda

All extracts from the works of Sri Aurobindo, the Mother and their disciples, as well as their photographs, have been reproduced with the kind permission of the Sri Aurobindo Ashram Trust.

First Edition 2012

ISBN No. 978-0-9562923-2-2

Copyright Sunayana Panda
Published by First Feature Ltd., London, UK
Produced by GBP Media, Pondicherry

Printed at Sri Aurobindo Ashram Press, Pondicherry
PRINTED IN INDIA

Cover design by Giles Herdman

This book is dedicated
to the one who loved books
and from whom
I have inherited
a love of history

CONTENTS

The Point of View of the Indian Leaders

The Point of View of the British

Preface

The story of how Sir Stafford Cripps came to India with a proposal from the British Government has often been told in the Ashram circle but rarely have the details been talked of or explained. We all know that this proposal was rejected by the Indian leaders of the time and that Sri Aurobindo was the only one who thought it should have been accepted. However, only a few know what exactly was in that proposal and why the leaders thought it was not worth accepting.

It is true that one should live with one's eyes trained on the future but sometimes it is important to understand the past because that knowledge helps us to better understand the present. Certain episodes of history have come down to us, retold by successive generations, as seen from one particular point of view. The passage of time allows us to have a look at the bigger picture and see the facts from another point of view, as well as to see facts that were not revealed earlier.

A part of the present compilation was first published in Mother India in its issue dated December 2008. I have added a few more chapters in order to give a more complete picture. It includes various points of view and accounts. There are several extracts and quotes which overlap and appear in more than one version of the story, but I have chosen to keep the repetitions in order to preserve the way the stories were told in the original version by each different narrator or writer. I have arranged the chapters in four clearly separate sections: an introduction, a section on the views of Sri Aurobindo, the Mother and some Ashram writers, this is followed by a section on the views of the Indian leaders and finally a section on the point of view of the British.

I would firstly like to draw the attention of the reading public to this chapter of Indian history which is not so widely known and secondly to give a more complete picture of this event. I would also like to point out how deeply Sri Aurobindo is connected to the history of India, how closely he watched the events that were unfolding in the world even though he did not step into the streets for more than 25 years. With his spiritual vision he could see the forces at play and he did all he could to help the Indian leaders take the right decision but they did not heed his advice.

It is easy to blame the Indian leaders of the time for the horrors of partition. It is time we looked at their own words and tried to understand why they took those decisions. They weighed the arguments for and against and finally chose, in good faith, the option that seemed to them to be the right one. It is also easy to believe that the British only wanted to divide and rule India, because we have been told so. Reading through the pages written by Winston Churchill himself and looking at the extracts from the diary of Sir Stafford Cripps it becomes clear that they were genuinely concerned for the people of India, not only during the war but also at the moment of the transfer of power. Perhaps through these essays the reader will come to be less judgemental and more compassionate towards those who had the fate of millions in their hands.

The ultimate aim of this work is to bring, in a simple and clear manner, the whole story of the Cripps Proposal to the devotees of Sri Aurobindo and the Mother, helping them to understand the details of this complex episode, which until

now was only within the grasp of the scholars and the histo-
rians.

While doing a part of my research at the British Library in
London, that temple of knowledge, I was often struck by the
thought that knowledge can be a great liberator. The more
we know the more we can rid ourselves of prejudices. There
is also a lot of truth in the old adage: "Time is a great healer".
Old enemies can with time become good friends. The young
who have grown up without prejudices can more easily accept the people of a country which was once an enemy of
their country. Having looked at the past and understood its
lessons it is best to forget the bitterness of colonisation and
partition, and to surge forward towards a more luminous future which is sure to flower into an age of human unity.

SUNAYANA PANDA

(*All the essays and extracts are taken from published sources,
except the three essays written by me. The reference of the source
has been given at the end of every chapter and the explanations
of particular words within a text appear in footnotes at the bot-
tom of the page.*)

INTRODUCTION

Sir Stafford Cripps

Who was Sir Stafford Cripps?

Sunayana Panda

All human knowledge is like a jigsaw puzzle. At first you know only a few things and by and by you add other bits of information because they connect with what you already know. It is a moment of great joy when you accidentally discover something which is a missing piece of the puzzle, and which connects two parts of knowledge you already have.

As I was looking at the books on the shelves of our local library in London my eyes fell on a biography of Sir Stafford Cripps. Was this the same Cripps to whom Sri Aurobindo had sent that famous telegram? Was this the same man who had replied with such dignity to him? Strange that we know next to nothing about Cripps although we can not stop repeating how the tragedy of the partition of India would never have happened if this man's proposal had been accepted by the leaders of the country in 1942.

I did not lose a minute and borrowed the book that day. The first thing I did was to look at the index in the hope of finding what his biographer might have said about his exchange of telegrams with Sri Aurobindo. No, he wasn't under 'S' and he wasn't under 'A'. Maybe he was classified under 'Ghose'? But he wasn't under that either. How could it be that a piece of information that was so important to us, the followers of Sri Aurobindo, was not even mentioned once in this exhaustive biography of Sir Stafford Cripps? Perhaps this is the sad truth, that no one actually registered how important that communication was.

We know that the national leaders did not think that Sri Aurobindo could advise them since he had left the field of active politics long before this incident. They may have imagined that a man who was immersed in his spiritual pursuits would not have understood the complexities of the issues at stake. Possibly they dismissed Duraiswami's visit and his verbal message as totally irrelevant to their work and this is why the whole incident has been lost from public memory. But I expected that at least Sir Stafford would have spoken of it to someone, that there had been at least one person who supported his proposal. Obviously, no one had taken note of that if he did mention it to anybody.

This biography, which is aptly called "The Cripps Version", is written by a historian who is a professor of Modern History at Cambridge University. If you think it is all academic jargon you are wrong because this biography reads like a novel and has a flowing language which can pull in a reader's interest. The book is almost entirely built up with the material the author has culled out of Sir Stafford's diaries. And it is not only one diary that we see the quotes from. An incident is often reconstructed from the point of view of several people who had all noted it in their diaries. One can assume that maintaining a diary was a very popular activity in Britain because we see paragraphs quoted from his children's diaries, his aunt's diaries as well as the diaries of his close associates and colleagues.

What kind of a man was Sir Stafford Cripps? What was his background and how important was he in his own country? I was even curious to know what he was like in his personal life. I have known his name since my school days and yet it was only when I saw the cover of this book did I actually see his face. I was amazed to find that there was so much to know about him but somehow he has remained just an undefined silhouette in our minds.

His real name was Richard Stafford Cripps, although somewhere in his early adult life he dropped the "Richard". Interesting to us is the fact that he was born in London on 24th April. The year he was born, 1889, Sri Aurobindo was in his final year at St. Paul's School. The street in Fulham where he was born in London is only a kilometre away from Cromwell Road where Sri Aurobindo was living at that time. Cripps was brought up in a privileged and aristocratic environment. He was keenly interested in science and did his M. Sc. from University College London although he had been accepted at Oxford. In actual fact, Oxford would have been a more advantageous choice considering that he wanted to eventually enter politics in later life. There he would have been able to make those crucial social contacts which are so necessary to the life of a politician but he chose University College London because it had better laboratory facilities. This may seem as a minor detail but essentially it shows that he was true to himself. Again interesting to us is the fact that he ended his student life after getting his M. Sc. in 1910, the year Sri Aurobindo left active politics and came to Pondicherry.

Stafford Cripps took up a career in law after getting a degree in science. This was only one of the many contradictions in his life. Although he was born into a wealthy family he chose to be a socialist and joined the Labour Party. He always stood out of the crowd. People were always baffled by the fact that he was a vegetarian, never drank and towards the latter part of his life gave up smoking. Today such a choice would seem the sensible thing to do but for British society of the 1930s this was considered something striking, because he belonged to the upper class and could afford to have the best of luxuries. At a time when most people could not even dream of possessing so much wealth he was willingly choosing to live a simple life.

He studied science because that was the natural bent of his mind and what truly interested him, but he took up law as a profession firstly because his family was already well-known in the legal circles and he could take over his father's practice but also because a legal experience was a sure road to a political career. Although it was his family connections that started off his law practice, in the end it was his own hard work that made him successful and famous. He could easily put in a 15-hour day. In fact, all his life he worked unusually long hours in spite of his unstable health. He suffered from digestive problems which were always aggravated when he was under stress.

His biographer notes, "The uncanny accuracy with which he could recollect and pinpoint relevant documents became the stuff of anecdotes." He became well-known for his phenomenal memory and for the way in which he held his cross-examination of the expert witnesses. He made sure that his preparation was flawless. "A Rolls-Royce mind, you knew as soon as you met him," this was a comment from one of his young admirers.

Had he never entered politics he would still have made his mark in England. Having a background in science he specialised in patent law. Very few lawyers of his time had that rare skill of having an equally deep knowledge of legal procedures as well as of science. By combining the knowledge of the two disciplines he made a contribution to the field of patent law by developing a means of evaluating the 'inventive step'. It demands that the inventor should be able to demonstrate that he is actually capable of manufacturing the product. This is still taught to law students as the "Cripps test".

In 1930 he became the Solicitor-General and was given the customary knighthood. Since then he was known as "Sir Stafford". He was also elected to the House of Commons, having already joined the Labour Party. By the early 1930s he was taking sure steps in his political career.

All these years, having only seen him mentioned in books connected with Sri Aurobindo, I had imagined that he had come only once to India, bearing in his hands the gift of his proposal which was rejected. From this biography I learnt that he had, in fact, come three times to India and always in connection with some mission or the other relating to the independence of the country. His relationship with India had started much before his first visit and continued well after the political ties had ended. It would indeed be a difficult task to go into all the details of what the Cripps Mission was and to go into an exhaustive discussion about why it failed. A rough idea of the situation however is necessary so that we can better understand why Sri Aurobindo went to such lengths to try and convince the decision makers of the merits of his proposal.

That famous 1942 visit was actually his second trip to India. The Second World War had reached a crucial point, the British had lost Singapore and Hong Kong and now the Japanese were almost at our doorstep. There was a pressing need to get India to participate in the war and to help the British to win it. The deal that Cripps wanted to strike on behalf of the British Government was that India would be given a Dominion Status in exchange for that help and it was understood that this status would eventually become self-government.

Stafford Cripps' first visit was in December 1939. It was

supposed to be an unofficial one but from the Indian side it was taken as seriously as an official trip. For Cripps the purpose was to get a first-hand view of the communal relations and to see how the different groups could be brought together to participate in the solutions that would eventually have to be worked out for the whole country. In India people were aware that he was seen by many in Britain as a possible future Prime Minister. His third visit in March 1946 was called the Cabinet Delegation and it was to chart out the details of the transfer of power in the context of the Indian independence. He tried his best to avoid partition but did not succeed.

Let us go back to that famous second visit. Sir Stafford Cripps came to India on 22nd March 1942 and on 11th April he announced officially that his offer had been rejected. This was a time when communications were slow and urgent messages were sent by telegram. Telephones existed but there were only a few of them and the connections were unreliable. Bearing this in mind it is really remarkable how quickly Sri Aurobindo took the step of sending him a message. That message is dated 31st March and begins with the words "I have heard your broadcast." This radio broadcast by Cripps was made on 30th March and it followed his press conference held on the 29th.

We know that during the war years Udar-da had a radio and that at the beginning, every day Pavita, the Englishwoman and Pavitra-da used to go to his house and note down in shorthand the news which was being broadcast, then write it out in longhand and maybe even type it out, then send it to Sri Aurobindo. At first the Mother did not want the radio to be brought to the Ashram but after a couple of years Udar-da insisted that they take it so that Sri Aurobindo could hear the news himself. In our present world of round- the-clock news flashing out of over a dozen TV channels in every house that the story of the radio being brought to the Ashram is almost out of a fairytale.

Considering that Sri Aurobindo had taken the unusual step of actually sending a telegram and an envoy to Sir Stafford the question that begs to be asked is, "Why was this proposal rejected?" Every party who was involved in it had a different answer to that question because it was a complex situation, but if we reduce it to a simple answer it would be that there was a great deal of misunderstanding and mistrust among the Indian leaders. Gandhi was against the war on grounds of non-violence, not realising the magnitude of Hitler's evil intentions. He was so sure that the British would lose the war that he even publicly commented that the Cripps proposal was a "post-dated cheque on a failing bank". One of the major stumbling blocks to the agreement was the matter of the leadership of the Indian Army, the other being the role of the Viceroy and the extent of his powers.

At this point let us take a look at the telegram sent by Sri Aurobindo to Sir Stafford:

I have heard your broadcast. As one who has been a nationalist leader and worker for India's independence though now my activity is no longer in the political but in the spiritual field, I wish to express my appreciation of all you have done to bring about this offer. I welcome it as an opportunity given to India to determine for herself and organise in all liberty of choice her freedom and unity and take an effective place among the world's free nations. I hope that it will be accepted and the right use made of it putting aside all discords and divisions. I hope too that a friendly relation between Britain and India replacing past struggles will be a step towards a greater world union in which as a free nation her spiritual force will contribute to build for mankind a better and happier life. In this light I offer my public adhesion in case it can be of any help in your work.

This message was sent on 31st March. Since it is written out in complete sentences it doesn't look like the usual telegram but it could not have been anything else because the answer to that is a telegram sent by Sir Stafford the very next day, 1st April 1942.

I AM MOST TOUCHED AND GRATIFIED BY YOUR KIND MESSAGE ALLOWING ME TO INFORM INDIA THAT YOU WHO OCCUPY UNIQUE POSITION IN IMAGINATION OF INDIAN YOUTH ARE CONVINCED THAT DECLARATION OF HIS MAJESTY'S GOVERN-MENT SUBSTATIALLY CONFERS THAT FREEDOM FOR WHICH INDIAN NATIONALISM HAS SO LONG STRUGGLED.

The most striking thing is that this exchange of messages is not mentioned in this detailed biography. Sir Stafford kept a diary in which he noted everything that happened to him and from which Peter Clarke, the biographer, quotes extensively. How strange that he has not written anything about this sole voice agreeing with him, coming from a remote corner of the country, from a small town governed by the French. Cripps stopped writing his diary after his last visit to India but before that he noted every personal observation, every impression and every hope and apprehension. It could also be that he did write about Sri Aurobindo's telegram in his diary but that the biographer did not consider it important enough to quote it in this book.

Sri Aurobindo did not stop at that message; he sent Duraiswami Iyer, the Madras lawyer, who was a disciple and an important member in the life of the Ashram, to go to Delhi as his emissary and to speak to the leaders. He also sent this telegram to C. Rajagopalachari who was in Delhi and was participating in these talks:

IS NOT COMPROMISE DEFENCE QUESTION BETTER THAN RUPTURE. SOME IMMEDIATE SETTLEMENT URGENT FACE GRAVE PERIL. HAVE SENT DURAI-SWAMI INSIST URGENCY. APPEAL TO YOU TO SAVE INDIA FORMIDABLE DANGER NEW FOREIGN DOMI-NATION WHEN OLD ON WAY TO SELF-ELIMINA-TION.

The fact that Rajagopalachari is mentioned as agreeing with the proposal is an indication that at least he could get that message to Cripps. In fact, let me quote Clarke's very words about that situation and we can see how faithfully he maintained what Sri Aurobindo had asked him to convey.

On the Congress side, Rajagopalachari spoke out prominently along these lines: refusing to blame Cripps himself, urging rapprochement with the Muslim League, and arguing that for Britain to quit India at its moment of peril from Japanese invasion would constitute betrayal.

After Cripps' departure the Indian leaders blamed him for the failure of the talks. Nehru, who had so far been seen as a friend of Sir Stafford, now openly criticised him. In fact,

Nehru had been very warm to Cripps' proposal at first and for a while it seemed as if the mission had been successful. But suddenly the tables turned at the last minute and it was formally rejected. Later Nehru said in a public speech, "I am happy that the negotiation failed and we were not caught in that snare." The situation became even more volatile and the Quit India movement was launched in August of that same year.

A peep into Nirod-da's *Twelve Years with Sri Aurobindo* reveals an interesting anecdote. After Cripps' mission was declared a failure Sri Aurobindo told those who were around him that he knew this mission would fail. They asked him why he had taken the trouble to send an emissary if he knew that it would fail. Nirod-da says, "He smiled in his usual enigmatic way, and said 'Well, I have done a bit of *nishkama karma* (disinterested work)'".

Cripps gradually rose from being the leader of the House of Commons in 1942 to the post of Chancellor of the Exchequer, the equivalent of the Finance Minister. During the War he was made a member of the War Cabinet and later the Minister of Aircraft Production. This must have been a particularly suitable post considering that he actually had constructed a life-size working model of one of those very early planes in the grounds of their country house when he was a teenager. As Chancellor of the Exchequer, a position he held from 1947, he worked unusually long hours, starting early in the morning. In the end he had to resign due to ill health and after two years of fighting against cancer he died in 1952 just three days before his 63rd birthday.

He is remembered as the rival of Churchill and his opposite in every way. While Churchill did not hide his strong reluctance to give independence to India, Cripps had always sympathised with India's desire for democracy. He was related to the India Conciliation group, made up of British people who supported the Indian freedom movement. Churchill was known to be fond of luxuries but Cripps believed in renouncing them. So much so that he was often referred to as "the English Gandhi". Churchill once said of him "He has all the virtues I dislike and none of the vices I admire."

It is something of a discovery to read that he had a strong inner life. He believed that "trying to remedy the inequalities in the world" was being faithful to the Christian teachings. He even wrote a book which he called *Towards Christian Democracy*. In 1948 in an address at the Westminster Chapel he spoke about his belief that the aim of life was to establish the Kingdom of God here on earth.

There is a diary entry from his early youth which gives us an indication about his inner reflections. He writes "…it is the re-genesis of the divine spirit which is needed and not a genesis. Every child is born with the same amount of divine spirit, that spirit may be crushed or it may be encouraged, or it may succeed or fail in spite of everything — but it can not die…" This is written in July 1910 when he was 21 years old.

He is remembered in England as "Austerity Cripps" because he advocated austerity in public spending. He took charge of the country's finances after the Second World War and tried to build it up. It was generally understood that he was extending to the life of the whole nation his personal preference for living austerely. The war had already brought a lot of hardships so people were not exactly pleased to deny themselves the good things of life even after the war had ended.

Since Cripps was born into a Christian culture he expressed his feelings in a Christian way. But clearly what he was seeking was something beyond religion. He wanted to bring to his country an ideal way of life. He was not interested in talking, what mattered to him was to see his thoughts turned into actions. To him his work in the outer world was directly connected to his progress in the inner world.

As I come to the final chapters of the book I realise that Peter Clarke, the author, has a style which is so engaging that what could easily have become a dull book about a British politician, who wasn't particularly colourful or witty, has turned out to be a fascinating volume about a man who was so closely connected with the independence of India. The author makes sure that the reader never loses sight of Cripps the man as he reads about Cripps the member of the War Cabinet or Cripps the Minister for Economic Affairs. The details of his innermost aspirations make the book worth reading.

Here is what Cripps wrote in his diary on 16th April 1946, when he was in India for the third time, regarding the transfer of power after Independence. After a day spent in talking to Jinnah and being unable to persuade him to change his stance.

> This is the really critical time and I feel personally that I must leave no stone unturned to get a favourable result for the future of 400 million people hangs in the balance in the next few days. May God give us wisdom to do what is right. I have never felt a heavier responsibility on my shoulders than just at this moment. I still feel we *must* succeed somehow. That is our duty and our debt to India…

Let us look into what he writes in his diary a few days later on 20th April 1946, which was Good Friday. This was written during a short break spent in Kashmir while the crucial talks were still on. Although it is a diary entry it was meant to be read by his wife Isobel.

> In the evening light it was a quite unforgettable sight. I had to wander off alone, it was too beautiful to share with anyone but you – it was that beauty which makes one happily sad – a deep sadness for humanity, an overwhelming sense of the smallness of man and his inability to cope with life…Somehow it seems peculiarly appropriate that this should be Eastertide and somehow this and Easter and our job all seem fitted in together – I am not sure how but I am sure that they are. This is perhaps God's answer to my and your prayers for guidance and out of this experience will come wisdom to deal with what is so intensely difficult a problem. I am sure that beauty and peace give wisdom and perhaps in the next 3 days God will give his guidance.

Behind the broad lines of history are individuals, made up of body, mind and heart – and a soul. We can gather from what he says in his telegram to Sri Aurobindo that he knew how he had inspired the nation towards independence. He probably didn't know more than that. How interesting it would have been for Cripps, on a personal level, if he had understood who Sri Aurobindo really was.

A few days after Sir Stafford's death his wife received a letter from Clementine Churchill, the wife of Winston Churchill, with the following words: "I know that Stafford was upheld by an intense spiritual life and an unshakable faith."

As I took the book back to return it I had one last glimpse at his photo. Here was a man I had heard so much about, who is almost a part of Ashram history, and yet I had been unaware of the most basic facts of his life. The more we know the more we discover that there is so much more to know, and every piece of knowledge is one more piece added in an infinite jigsaw puzzle.

Reference

All quotations are from *The Cripps Version: The Life of Sir Stafford Cripps* by Peter Clarke published by Penguin, 2002.

Quotations from Sri Aurobindo as well as the telegraphic message from Cripps are from *Autobiographical Notes and Other Writings of Historical Interest* published by Sri Aurobindo Ashram, Pondicherry, 2006.

Sri Aurobindo

The Broadcast by Sir Stafford Cripps

30th March 1942

I want tonight to give you a short explanation of the document which was published in the Press this morning, and which gives the proposals of the British War Cabinet for the future of India, a document unanimously agreed upon by every member of that Cabinet.

First of all you will want to know what object we had in view. Well, we wanted to make it quite clear and beyond any possibility of doubt or question that the British Government and the British people desire the Indian peoples to have full self-government, with a constitution as free in every respect as our own in Great Britain or as of any of the great Dominion members of the British Commonwealth of Nations. In the words of the draft Declaration, India would be, "associated with the United Kingdom and other dominions by a common allegiance to the Crown but equal to them in every respect, in no way subordinate in any aspect of its domestic or external affairs".

There is however an existing constitution which regulates the central and provincial Governments of India and everyone agrees that in these troublous times we cannot here and now set about forging a new Constitution. It is far too important a matter for the future of India to be improvised in a hurried way.

The principle on which these proposals are based is that the new Constitution should be framed by the elected representatives of the Indian peoples themselves, so we propose that immediately hostilities are ended a Constitution-making body should be set up consisting of elected repre-sentatives from British India, and if the Indian States wish, as we hope they will, to become part of the new Indian Union, they too will be invited to send their representatives to this Constitution-making body, though, if they do, that will not, of itself, bind them to become members of the Union. That is the broad outline of the future.

Now what is to happen in the meantime?

The British people are determined to do their utmost for the defence of India and we are confident that in that great task the Indian peoples of all races and religions are eager to play their full part.

Let me read to you what the statement says on this point —

> "(e) During the critical period which now faces India and until the new Constitution can be framed, His Majesty's Government must inevitably bear the responsibility for and retain the control and direction of the defence of India as part of their world war effort, but the task of organising to the full the military, moral and material resources of India must be the responsibility of the Government of India with the co-operation of the peoples of India. His Majesty's Government desire and invite the immediate and effective participation of the leaders of the principal sections of the Indian people in the counsels of their country, of the Commonwealth and of the United Nations. Thus they will be enabled to give their active and constructive help in the discharge of a task which is vital and essential for the future freedom of India". So ends the document.

The Governor-General, whose task it is to form the Central

Government of India, has done his utmost to assist me with my mission, and I am certain that the Indian leaders can rely upon him to find the best way in consultation with them for carrying out the general principle laid down in the clause that I have just read to you.

So much for the general framework of the proposals. But, as we all know, the most vital and difficult question is that which concerns the interests of the various communities amongst the Indian peoples.

I will not attempt to go into any of the historical origins of these difficulties, let us instead look at them as a present fact. In the great sub-continent of India there is more than one people, there are many peoples and races as there are in the great sub-continent of Russia. Our object is to give to the Indian peoples full self-government with complete freedom as to how they will devise and organise their own Constitution.

There are those who claim that India should form a single united country, there are others who say it should be divided up into two, three or more separated countries. There are those who claim that Provincial Autonomy should be very wide with but few centrally controlled federal services; others stress the need for centralisation in view of the growing complexity of economic development.

These and many other and various ideas are worthy to be explored and debated, but it is for the Indian peoples, and not for any outside authority, to decide under which of these forms India will in the future govern herself.

If the Indian peoples ask our help it will of course be gladly given but it is for you, the Indian peoples, to discuss and decide upon your future Constitution. We shall look on with deep interest and hope that your wisdom will guide you truly in this great adventure.

We ask you, therefore, to come together — all religions and races — in a Constitution-making body as soon as hostilities are over to frame your own Constitution.

We have specified the form which that body will take, unless, and this is an important point, the leaders of the principal sections of Indian opinion agree between themselves before the end of hostilities upon some other and better form.

That Constitution-making body will have as its object the framing of a single Constitution for the whole of India — that is, of British India together with such of the Indian States as may decide to join in.

But we realise this very simple fact. If you want to persuade a number of people who are inclined to be antagonistic to enter the same room, it is unwise to tell them that once they go in there is no way out — they are to be forever locked in together.

It is much wiser to tell them they can go in and if they find they can't come to a common decision, then there is nothing to prevent those who wish, from leaving again by another door. They are much more likely all to go in if they have knowledge that they can by their free will go out again if they cannot agree.

Well, that is what we say to the Provinces of India. Come together to frame a common Constitution — if you find after all your discussion and all the give and take of a Constitution-making assembly that you cannot overcome your differences and that some Provinces are still not satisfied with the Constitution, then such Provinces can go out and remain out if they wish and just the same degree of self-government and freedom will be available for them as for the Union itself, that is to say complete self-government.

We hope and expect to see an Indian Union, strong and united, because it is founded upon the free consent of all its peoples; but it is not for us Britishers to dictate to you, the Indian peoples, you will work out and decide that problem for yourselves.

So we provide the means and the road by which you can attain that form of the absolute and united self-government that you desire at the earliest possible moment. In the past we have waited for the different Indian communities to come to a common decision as to how a new Constitution for a self-governing India should be framed and because there has been no agreement amongst the Indian leaders, the British Government has been accused by some of using this fact to delay the granting of freedom to India. We are now giving the lead that has been asked for and it is in the hands of Indians and Indians only whether they will accept that lead and so attain their own freedom. If they fail to accept this opportunity the responsibility for that failure must rest with them.

We ask you to accept this fulfilment of our pledges in the past and it is that request that I have put before your leaders in the document which you have now seen.

As regards the position of minority communities within the new Indian Union, I am confident that the Constitution-making body will make just provision for their protection. But in view of the undertakings given to these minorities by His Majesty's Government in the past we propose that in the Treaty which, under the draft Declaration, will be concluded between His Majesty's Government and the Constitution-making body, the new Indian Union should undertake to protect the rights of these minorities If there should be any non-acceding Provinces a similar

Treaty provision would be made in respect of minority communities within their borders.

I have already indicated to you the position as to the immediate future.

I know that His Excellency the Viceroy has the greatest hope that the acceptance in   principle of this document by the leaders of Indian opinion will make it possible for him to start forthwith upon the consultations which will enable him to implement the principle laid down in the last paragraph of the document which I have already read over to you.

It contains one essential reservation — that in respect of the responsibility for Defence. This reservation does not mean that the Governor-General and his Executive Council will or indeed could be excluded from taking an effective share in the counsels for the defence of India. In this wide-flung war, defence cannot be localised in a single country and its preparation must permeate the activities of every department of Government and must demand from every department the fullest co-operation. If His Majesty's Government are to take full responsibility for the conduct of the naval, military and air defence of India, as it is their duty to do, then the defence of India must be dealt with by them as part of the world war effort in which they are now engaged, and the direction of that defence must rest in the hands of the Commander-in-Chief under the War Cabinet and their highest staff officers. But, as I have already pointed out, the Government of India must also have an effective share in the Defence counsels and so we have decided that the Commander-in-Chief must retain his position as a Member of the Executive Council.

In order, however, that India may have her full voice in this central control of strategy, defensive and offensive, not only in India itself but in all the interrelated theatres of war, we have invited the appointment of a representative Indian to the War Cabinet and to the Pacific Council of the United Nations[1] — that is one of the ways in which India will have her full say in the counsels of the Commonwealth and of the United Nations as an equal partner. And when it comes to the making of the peace, India will appoint her own representatives to the Peace Conference side by side with those of the other free Nations and so make her contribution to the building of a new world order.

I am confident that nothing further or more complete could be done towards the immediate realisation of the just claims and demands of the Indian peoples. Our proposals are definite and precise. If they were to be rejected by the leaders of Indian opinion, there would be neither the time nor the opportunity to reconsider this matter till after the war and it would be a bitter blow to the friends of India all over the world.

I consider it a high honour that it has fallen to my lot to be the messenger of the War Cabinet in a matter of such vital and far-reaching importance to the future world order. I personally am convinced of the soundness and completeness of these proposals, and I have asked your leaders to give to them an ungrudging acceptance.

There will still be difficulties perhaps — the result of the distrust which has grown up between us in past years, but I ask you to turn your back upon the past, to accept my hand, our hand of friendship and trust and to allow us to join with you for the time being in working to establish and complete

1. The term 'United Nations' was coined by Roosevelt during the Second World War to denote the Allied Forces.

your freedom and your self-government. This as you may know has long been a cause dear to my heart and it is with the greatest hopes that I look to the events of the next few days which may if wisely handled seal for ever your freedom and our friendship.

Your country today is in peril from a cruel aggressor, an aggressor whose hand has soaked in blood and suffering great areas of China with its friendly and democratic peoples, an aggressor allied to those nations who have deluged with tragedy the once peaceful plains of Russia. Against those aggressors we and the allied nations will fight to victory.

The outlook is overcast for the moment, but believe me, I have no doubt as to the final result. Russia, the United States, China and Great Britain have resources which the axis and its allies can never defeat.

We stand by our duty growing out of our past historical associations, to give you every protection that we can, but with your willing help and co-operation this can be made more effective and more powerful.

Let us enter upon this primary task of the defence of India in the now sure knowledge that when we emerge from the fire and travail of war it will be to build a free India upon foundations wrought by the Indian peoples themselves, and to forge a long lasting and free friendship between our two peoples. Regrets and recriminations as to the past can have no place beside the confident and sure hopes of the future, when a free India will take her rightful place a co-worker with the other free nations in that world reconstruction which alone can make the toil and suffering of the war worth while.

Let the dead past bury its dead! And let us march together side by side through the night of high endeavour and courage to the already waking dawn of a new world of liberty for all the peoples.

Reference

The Cripps Mission, edited by Sukhamay Banerjee and Shanti Mitra, published by Bamabo, Calcutta, October 1942, pp.32-38.

The Telegram sent by Sri Aurobindo to Sir Stafford Cripps and the Reply

31st March 1942

Sir Stafford Cripps
New Delhi

I have heard your broadcast. As one who has been a nationalist leader and worker for India's independence though now my activity is no longer in the political but in the spiritual field, I wish to express my appreciation of all you have done to bring about this offer. I welcome it as an opportunity given to India to determine for herself and organise in all liberty of choice her freedom and unity and take an effective place among the world's free nations. I hope that it will be accepted and the right use made of it putting aside all discords and divisions. I hope too that a friendly relation between Britain and India replacing past struggles will be a step towards a greater world union in which as a free nation her spiritual force will contribute to build for mankind a better and happier life. In this light I offer my public adhesion in case it can be of any help in your work.

Sri Aurobindo
The Ashram
Pondicherry

Sir Stafford Cripps's Telegram in Reply

1st April 1942

I AM MOST TOUCHED AND GRATIFIED BY YOUR KIND MESSAGE ALLOWING ME TO INFORM INDIA THAT YOU WHO OCCUPY UNIQUE POSITION IN IMAGINATION OF INDIAN YOUTH ARE CONVINCED THAT DECLARATION OF HIS MAJESTY'S GOVERNMENT SUBSTANTIALLY CONFERS THAT FREEDOM FOR WHICH INDIAN NATIONALISM HAS SO LONG STRUGGLED.

STAFFORD CRIPPS

THE POINT OF VIEW OF
THE ASHRAM

References in Sri Aurobindo's Writings About The Cripps Proposal

(The texts in this chapter are written by Sri Aurobindo even though he refers to himself in the third person. When answering letters to people outside the Ashram Sri Aurobindo often wrote notes to his secretary who then translated or paraphrased his replies and sent them to the correspondent under his own signature. In such cases Sri Aurobindo wrote about himself in the third person.)

At no time did he consent to have anything to do with the sham Reforms which were all the Government at that period cared to offer. He held up always the slogan of "no compromise" or, as he now put it in his Open Letter to his countrymen published in the *Karmayogin*, "no co-operation without control". It was only if real political, administrative and financial control were given to popular ministers in an elected Assembly that he would have anything to do with offers from the British Government. Of this he saw no sign until the proposal of the Montagu Reforms in which first something of the kind seemed to appear. He foresaw that the British Government would have to begin trying to meet the national aspiration half-way, but he would not anticipate that moment before it actually came. The Montagu Reforms came nine years after Sri Aurobindo had retired to Pondicherry and by that time he had abandoned all outward and public political activity in order to devote himself to his spiritual work, acting only by his spiritual force on the movement in India, until his prevision of real negotiations between the British Government and the Indian leaders was fulfilled by the Cripps proposal and the events that came after.

(*Autobiographical Notes and Other Writings of Historical Interest,*
pp. 62-63)

*

His retirement from political activity was complete, just as was his personal retirement into solitude in 1910.

But this did not mean, as most people supposed, that he had retired into some height of spiritual experience devoid of any further interest in the world or in the fate of India. It could not mean that, for the very principle of his Yoga was not only to realise the Divine and attain to a complete spiritual consciousness, but also to take all life and all world activity into the scope of this spiritual consciousness and action and to base life on the Spirit and give it a spiritual meaning. In his retirement Sri Aurobindo kept a close watch on all that was happening in the world and in India and actively intervened whenever necessary, but solely with a spiritual force and silent spiritual action; for it is part of the experience of those who have advanced far in Yoga that besides the ordinary forces and activities of the mind and life and body in Matter, there are other forces and powers that can act and do act from behind and from above; there is also a spiritual dynamic power which can be possessed by those who are advanced in spiritual consciousness, though all do not care to possess or, possessing, to use it, and this power is greater than any other and more effective. It was this force which, as soon as he had attained to it, he used, at first only in a limited field of personal work, but afterwards in a constant action upon the world forces. He had no reason to be dissatisfied with the results or to feel the necessity of any other kind of action. Twice however he found it advisable to take in addition other action of a public kind. The first was in relation to the Second World War. At the beginning he did not actively concern himself with it, but when it appeared as if Hitler would crush all the forces opposed to him and Nazism dominate the world, he began to intervene. He declared himself publicly on the side of the Allies, made some financial contributions in answer to the appeal for funds and encouraged those who sought his advice to enter the army or share in the war effort. Inwardly, he put his spiritual force behind the Allies from the moment of Dunkirk when everybody was expecting the immediate fall of England and the definite triumph of Hitler, and he had the satisfaction of seeing the rush of German victory almost immediately arrested and the tide of war begin to turn in the opposite direction. This he did, because he saw that behind Hitler and Nazism were dark Asuric forces and that their success would mean the enslavement of mankind: to the tyranny of evil, and a set-back to the course of evolution and especially to the spiritual evolution of mankind; it would lead also to the enslavement not only of Europe but of Asia, and in it India, an enslavement far more terrible than any this country had ever endured, and the undoing of all the work that had been done for her liberation. It was this reason also that induced him to support publicly the Cripps offer and to press the Congress leaders to accept it. He had not, for various reasons, intervened with his spiritual force against the Japanese aggression until it became evident that Japan intended to attack and even invade and conquer India. He allowed certain letters he had written in support of the war affirming his views of the Asuric nature and inevitable outcome to Hitlerism to become public. He supported the Cripps offer because by its acceptance India and Britain could stand united against the Asuric forces and the solution of Cripps could be used as a step towards independence. When negotiations failed, Sri Aurobindo returned to his reliance on the use of spiritual force alone against the aggressor and had the satisfaction of seeing the tide of Japanese victory, which had till then swept everything before it, changed immediately into a tide of rapid, crushing and finally immense and overwhelming defeat. He had also after a time the satisfaction of seeing his previsions about the future of India justify themselves so that she stands independent with whatever internal difficulties.

(*Ibid.*, pp. 65-66)

*

It was not till Provincial Autonomy was conceded that he felt a real change in the British attitude had begun; the Cripps offer he accepted as a further progress in that change and the final culmination in the Labour Government's new policy as its culmination.

(*Ibid.*, p. 87)

*

As for the Cripps offer, it was supported in a long telegram sent not to the Viceroy's Secretary but to Cripps himself after his broadcast in which he announced the offer.

(*Ibid.*, p. 104)

*

Sri Aurobindo does not know whether this can be described as a public political gesture.

(Ibid.)

Telegrams From Sri Aurobindo

(Note given to Duraiswamy Iyer for Congress Working Committe)

In view of the urgency of the situation I am sending Mr. Duraiswamy Iyer to convey my views on the present negotiations and my reasons for pressing on Indian leaders the need of a settlement. He is accredited to speak for me.

April 1, 1942   (*Ibid.*, p. 470)

*

(Telegram to Dr. B. S. Moonje)

DR. MOONJE HINDU MAHASABHA NEW DELHI

SETTLEMENT INDIA BRITAIN URGENT, FACE APPROACH GRAVE PERIL MENACING FUTURE INDIA. IS THERE NO WAY WHILE RESERVING RIGHT REPUDIATE RESIST PARTITION MOTHERLAND TO ACCEPT CO-OPERATION PURPOSE WAR INDIA UNION. CANNOT COMBINATION MAHASABHA CONGRESS NATIONALIST AND ANTI-JINNAH MUSLIM DEFEAT LEAGUE IN ELECTIONS BENGAL PUNJAB SIND. HAVE SENT ADVOCATE DURAISWAMI IYER TO MEET YOU.

2 April 1942   (*Ibid.*)

*

(*Telegram to C. Rajagopalachari*)

RAJAGOPALACHARI BIRLA HOUSE NEW DELHI

IS NOT COMPROMISE DEFENCE QUESTION BET-
TER THAN RUPTURE. SOME IMMEDIATE SETTLE-
MENT URGENT FACE GRAVE PERIL. HAVE SENT DU-
RASWAMI INSIST URGENCY. APPEAL TO YOU TO SAVE
INDIA FORMIDABLE DANGER NEW FOREIGN DOMI-
NATION WHEN OLD ON WAY TO SELF-ELIMINATION.
2 April 1942   (*Ibid.*)

*

(*Telegram to Amarendra Chatterjee*)

AMARENDRA CHATTERJEE M. L. A. DELHI

UNABLE LEAVE PONDICHERRY. AWAITING CON-
GRESS DECISION NECESSARY FOR TOTAL NATION
ACTION. HAVE APPEALED PRIVATELY CONGRESS
LEADERS FOR UNDERSTANDING WITH BRITAIN AND
FIGHT DEFENCE INDIA.
9 April 1942   (*Ibid.,* p. 471)

*

(*Second Telegram to Amarendra Chatterjee*)

MY BLESSINGS ON YOUR EFFORTS TO SERVE AND
DEFEND MOTHERLAND NOW IN DANGER.

(*Ibid.*)

Nirodbaran

Amal Kiran

A Bit of *Nishkama Karma*

Nirodbaran

When Gandhi complained that the Viceroy did not say anything in reply to all his questions, Sri Aurobindo said to us in one of our talks on October 7th, 1940: "What will he say? It is very plain why he did not. First of all, the Government doesn't want to concede the demand for independence. What it is willing to give is Dominion Status after the War, expecting that India will settle down into a common relationship with the Empire. But just now a national government will virtually mean Dominion Status with the Viceroy only as a constitutional head. Nobody knows what the Congress will do after it gets power. It may be occupied only with India's defence and give such help as it can spare to England. And if things go wrong with the British, it may even make a separate peace leaving them in the lurch. There are Left Wingers, Socialists, Communists whom the Congress won't be able to bring to its side, neither will it dare to offend them and if their influence is sufficiently strong, the Congress may stand against the British. Thus it is quite natural for them not to part with power just now as it is also natural for us to make our claims. But since we haven't got even strength to back us, we have to see if we have any common meeting ground with the Government. If there is, a compromise is the only practical step. There was such an opportunity, but the Congress spoiled it. Now you have to accept what you get or I don't know what is going to happen. Of course, if we have the strength and power to make a revolution and get what we want, it would be a different matter. Amery and others did offer Dominion Status at one time. Now they have changed their position because they have come to know the spirit of our people. Our politicians have some fixed idea and they always go by them. Politicians and statesmen have to take account of situations and act as demanded by them. They must have insight."

"But it is because of the British divide-and-rule policy that we can't unite," we parried.

"Nonsense!"[1] Sri Aurobindo rebuffed. "Was there unity in India before the British rule?...Does Jinnah want unity? His very character shows what he wants — independence for the Muslims and rule over India if possible. The old spirit."

In the impasse created partially by the bankruptcy of the Congress policy, Providence came to the rescue in the form of the Cripps' Proposal which, if accepted would have changed the fate of India. But the forces of distrust, discontent and wanting everything at once, led to a failure to see the substance of Swaraj, as Sri Aurobindo has said, in the offer. There was a pother about small points and overlooking of the central important objective to be attained. Sri Aurobindo found in the proposal a fine opportunity for the solution of India's intricate problems and her ultimate liberation.

We may note that the Proposal envisaged a single, free, undivided India setting up a united front against the enemy. He promptly sent a message to Sir Stafford Cripps welcoming the Proposal and recommended its acceptance to the Indian leaders. The message was as follows:

"I have heard your broadcast. As one who has been a

---

1. Sri Aurobindo meant not that the British never followed the policy of divide-and-rule, but that divisions were already there for them to take advantage of and increase.

nationalist leader and worked for India's independence though now my activity is no longer in the political but in the spiritual field, I wish to express my appreciation of all you have done to bring about this offer. I welcome it as an opportunity given to India to determine for herself and organise in all liberty of choice her freedom and unity and take an effective place among the world's free nations. I hope that it will be accepted and the right use made of it putting aside all discords and divisions. I hope too that a friendly relation between Britain and India replacing past struggles will be a step towards a greater world union in which as a free nation her spiritual force will contribute to build for mankind a better and happier life. In this light I offer my public adhesion in case it can be of any help to your work."

Sir Stafford Cripps replied,

"I am most touched and gratified by your kind message allowing me to inform India that you who occupy unique position in imagination of Indian youth are convinced that declaration of His Majesty's Government substantially confers that freedom for which Indian Nationalism has so long struggled."

Sri Aurobindo also sent messages through Mr Shiva Rao to Mahatma Gandhi and Pandit Nehru that Cripps' offer should be accepted unconditionally. Lastly, he sent his envoy to Delhi to appeal to the Congress leaders for its acceptance, for sanity and wisdom to prevail. At this crucial moment Sri Aurobindo could not remain a passive witness to the folly that was about to be committed. His seer-vision saw that the Proposal had come on a wave of divine inspiration. The scene is still fresh in our memory. It was the evening hour. Sri Aurobindo was sitting on the edge of his bed just before his daily walking exercise. All of us were present; Duraiswami, the distinguished Madras lawyer and disciple was selected as the envoy, perhaps because he was a friend of Rajagopalachari, one of the prominent Congress leaders. He was to start for Delhi that very night. He came for Sri Aurobindo's blessings, lay prostrate before him, got up and stood looking at the Master with folded hands and then departed.

We may remind ourselves of Talthybius' mission to Troy in Sri Aurobindo's epic poem *Ilion*.(…) Similarly, Duraiswami went with India's soul in his frail hands and brought it back, downhearted, rewarded with ungracious remarks for the gratuitous advice. Sri Aurobindo even sent a telegram to Rajagopalachari and Dr Moonje urging them to accept the Proposal. (…) Cripps flew back a disappointed man but with the consolation and gratified recognition that at least one great man had welcomed the idea. When the rejection was announced, Sri Aurobindo said in a quiet tone, "I knew it would fail." We at once pounced on him and asked him, "Why did you then send Duraiswami at all?" "For a bit of *nishkama karma*,"[1] was his calm reply, without any bitterness or resentment. The full spirit of the kind of 'disinterested work' he meant he comes out in an early letter of his — (December 1933), which refers to his spiritual work, "I am sure of the results of my work. But even if I still saw the chance that it might come to nothing (which is impossible), I would go on unperturbed, because I would still have done to the

---

1. Disinterested work, the essence of which is that the work is inwardly dedicated to the Divine with no attchment to the result.

best of my power the work that I had to do, and what is so done always counts in the economy of the universe."

(…)

We know the aftermath of the rejection of the Cripps' Proposal: confusion, calamity, partition, blood-bath etc., and the belated recognition of the colossal blunder. Then when the partition had been accepted as a settled fact, Sri Aurobindo's 'bardic' voice was heard once again, "But by whatever means, in whatever way, the division must go; unity must and will be achieved, for it is necessary for the greatness of India's future."

Past events have justified Sri Aurobindo's solemn warning and recent events point to the way to the liquidation of that division.[1]

Reference

This extract is taken from Nirodbaran's book *Twelve Years with Sri Aurobindo* published by Sri Aurobindo Ashram, 2010 (pp139-145)

1. We are happy to see that Sri Aurobindo's prediction has been half-fulfilled for Bangladesh (East Pakistan) is now entirely independent.

Mention of Sir Stafford Cripps in *Evening Talks*

Sri Aurobindo had sent a message to the Congress regarding the Cripps Proposal.

Disciple: There are some people who even try to maintain that you knew fully well that your message to the Congress would fail and yet you sent it.

Sri Aurobindo: Yes, I knew that there was very little chance of its success.

Disciple: But suppose you had known that it would certainly fail, then in that case you might have spared the trouble of going and coming to Doraiswamy.

Sri Aurobindo: No, even if I had known for a certainty that it would fail, still it had to be done. It is a question of the play of forces and the important thing is that the other force should not be there. We cannot explain these things – this play of forces – to people who ask for a rational explanation, because it is so 'irrational'!

7th August 1943

C. Rajagopalachari in the Puja issue of the *Amrita Bazar Patrika* has pleaded for the reconsideration and revival of the Cripps proposals. Sri Aurobindo found this comment "late" but remarked that C.R. had got back his clarity of mind. As to the actual revival, when Wavell comes the difficulties he will face will be the I.C.S. and the Congress on two sides, and Jinnah on a third.

4th October 1943

Reference

Evening Talks with Sri Aurobindo recorded by A. B. Purani
Published by Sri Aurobindo Ashram, Pondicherry, Fourth Edition 2007, pp. 769-70

Sri Aurobindo

The Background of the Cripps Mission

K. R. Srinivasa Iyengar

In the early years of Japan's career of aggression — first in Manchuria, then in China – Sri Aurobindo didn't seem to attach much importance to it. But things assumed a different complexion when, after the eruption of the War in Europe, Subhash Chandra Bose escaped from India, established contacts with the Nazi and Japanese leaders, and organised the Indian National Army on foreign soil for the liberation of India from the British yoke with the aid of Japanese arms. After Japan's entry into the War against Britain and the USA, Subhash Bose's broadcasts to India, and the fall of Singapore and Rangoon, people in India were perhaps even more confused than before. While Gandhiji and the Congress leaders advised only withholding of support to the British war effort in India, the INA asked for active all-out resistance to the British Government in India. This was a further serious complicating factor, and as the first months of 1942 registered a series of spectacular Japanese victories, many in India — in their flawed knowledge and half-ignorance — began to feel and even hoped that British power would soon collapse in India too, and that the INA and the Japanese supporting army would accomplish their "chalo Dilli!" plan of conquest. But Sri Aurobindo had no doubt whatsoever that the winning of freedom with Japanese help was *not* the way to solve India's problem, and he declared:

Japan's imperialism being young and based on industrial and military power and moving westward, was a greater menace to India than the British imperialism which was old, which the country had learnt to deal with and which was on the way to elimination.

[….]

…As Japanese arms steadily advanced in the Pacific and Indian Ocean expanses, overrunning Malaysia and the Dutch East Indies, and as the War approached the shores of India, on 11 March 1942 Churchill offered to create a new Indian Union with a Dominion Constitution to be framed by India's own representatives after the War. In the meantime, the Indian leaders were invited to join a responsible Central Government and help the allied war effort. When presently Sir Stafford Cripps arrived in India to work out the details of an Indo-British concord Sri Aurobindo extended an open welcome to him on 31 March 1942….

[….]

While such was Sri Aurobindo's reaction — which was also the Mother's — to the Cripps Mission, some of the sadhaks were critical. The day after Cripps' broadcast, there was a discussion in Pavitra's room, and the Mother happening to come that side, joined the group and spoke her mind with supernal calm. Although an exact account is not available, she is reported by one of the group to have said:

One should leave the matter of Cripps' offer entirely in the hands of the Divine, with full confidence that the Divine will work everything out. Certainly there were flaws in the offer. Nothing on earth created by man is flawless, because the human mind has a limited capacity. Yet behind this offer there is the Divine Grace directly present. The Grace is now at the door of India, ready to give its help… But if it is rejected the Grace will withdraw and then the nation will suffer terribly, calamity will overtake it.

The Mother then referred to France rejecting Grace in 1940 when Churchill, after the evacuation from Dunkirk, offered a 'union' and joint nationality with Britain to fight Hitler, the common enemy. The Grace withdrew, and the soul of France went down:

But India, with her background of intense spiritual development through the ages, must realise the Grace is behind this offer…My ardent request to India is that she should not reject it. She must not make the same mistake that France has done recently…

Later in the day, the sadhaks came to know about Sri Aurobindo's message to Cripps (in response to his broadcast) and his telegraphic reply. But not content with his public espousal, Sri Aurobindo also sent Duraiswami Iyer as his personal emissary to the Congress Working Committee then holding its meeting in Delhi. Sri Aurobindo's (and the Mother's) point of view was that India had more to fear from Japanese imperialism than from the British, which after all was on its way out. It would be advisable to get into the seats of power now that the chance had come, without squeamishly arguing about the exact legal basis of that power. The Cripps Proposal also offered an opportunity for Hindus and Muslims to work together and thereby once and for all lay to rest the ghost of the "Two Nations" theory. And, above all, it was necessary to organise the collective strength of the country and repel the very real danger from Japan.

But it was all to no purpose. Gandhiji had described the Cripps Plan as "a post-dated cheque on a bank that was crashing"; and that was enough for the Congress leaders! Since Britain's was quite obviously the losing side, why then rush to its support? The Congress thus shied away from the invitation to join the Central Government. Divine wisdom was cavalierly vetoed by short-sighted political calculation, the proffered Grace was spurned, and the possibility of a free *and* united India was jeopardised irreparably. On coming to know about the rejection of the Cripps Proposal, the Mother only said out of the sadness of her heart and her infallible occult perception: "Now calamity will befall India." Years later, K. M. Munshi was to say in the course of a speech in Delhi on 16th August 1951:

> He [Sri Aurobindo] saw into the heart of things… when the whole country wanted to maintain neutrality, it was he of the unerring eye who said that the triumph of England and France was the triumph of the divine forces over the demonic forces. We were very angry, but it was a fact…He spoke again when Sir Stafford Cripps came with his first proposal… We rejected the advice…but today we realise that if the first proposal had been accepted, there would have been no partition, no refugees and no Kashmir problem.

Certainly, after the rejection of the Cripps offer, the situation in India was grim enough, whichever way one looked at it. In their perverse purblindness the Congress leaders, not only rejected the Grace that came with the Cripps offer, but they also queered the political pitch by mouthing aggressive slogans and adopting uncompromising postures. The leaders were obviously confused, and the mass of the people even more so; and things came to a point of no return when, in August 1942, spurning the seasoned appeals of statesmen like Rajagopalachari, the Congress under Gandhiji launched the Quit India movement.

Reference

On The Mother by K. R. Srinivasa Iyengar, published by Sri Aurobindo International Centre of Education, Pondicherry, revised edition 1994, pp 424-427

Sri Aurobindo and The Cripps Proposal

Amal Kiran (K.D. Sethna)

The end of March and the beginning of April 1942 are memorable for one of the very few interventions of Sri Aurobindo in India's public affairs. World War II was in full swing and Japan had joined hands with Hitler and posed a threat to Burma and even India, both of which were then under British rule. There was considerable discontent in India and a great reluctance to join the war effort of the British Commonwealth. India could not see much difference between German Nazism and British Imperialism. Most people forget that the latter was the gradually fading remnant of an old turn of the human political mind, which had once played a necessary role in history but had lost its *raison d'être* in the modern age of national freedom, whereas the former with its dogmas of master race and absolute dictator and merciless regimentation was a current contrary to the drive of human evolution with its many-sided variation both individual and collective.

Churchill was England's Prime Minister at the time. He had been known as a die-hard Imperialist. All of a sudden he appeared to have felt that in the war he was conducting against Hitler the cause of civilisation was at stake and that to serve it at all costs was more important than to preserve the sanctity of the British Empire. He wanted India to give up her distrust of the British and throw in her lot wholeheartedly with Britain's own valiant effort to fight the barbarism that was on the march from Germany under the emblem of the Swastika. He gave ear to the advice of liberal thought in

England which was in favour of conceding greater freedom to India that had been agitating for independence, especially since the days when Sri Aurobindo had become for a few years the leader of the Nationalist Movement. The well-known liberal thinker, Sir Stafford Cripps, was prominent as a spokesman of this advice. Churchill chose him to carry to India certain proposals meant to meet her basic demands and induce her to join the united front of Britain and her allies against Hitler and his associates. In connection with what came to be known as the Cripps Proposals it may be interesting to put together all the documents relating to Sri Aurobindo's intervention.

Sir Stafford, on arriving in India, issued the following Draft Declaration on behalf of the British Government:

> His Majesty's Government, having considered the anxieties expressed in this country and in India as to the fulfilment of promises made in regard to the future of India, have decided to lay down in precise and clear terms the steps which they propose shall be taken for the earliest possible realisation of self-government in India. The object is the creation of a new Indian Union which shall constitute a Dominion associated with the United Kingdom and other Dominions by a common allegiance to the Crown but equal to them in every respect, in no way subordinate in any aspect of its domestic and external affairs.

On hearing this declaration on the radio, Sri Aurobindo had the insight that the offer sent by Churchill through Sri Stafford Cripps had come on the wave of a divine inspiration and that it gave India the substance of independence. At once he sent a telegram to Sir Stafford:

> I have heard your broadcast. As one who has been a nationalist leader and worker for India's independence though now my activity is no longer in the political but I the spiritual field, I wish to express my appreciation of all you have done to bring about this offer. I welcome it as an opportunity given to India to determine for herself and organise in all liberty of choice her freedom and unity and take an effective place among the world's free nations. I hope that it will be accepted and the right use made of it putting aside all discords and divisions. I hope too that a friendly relation between Britain and India replacing past struggles will be a step towards a greater world union in which as a free nation her spiritual force will contribute to build for mankind a better and happier life. In this light I offer my public adhesion in case it can be of any help in your work. (March 31, 1942)

Cripps immediately telegraphed back to Sri Aurobindo:

> I AM MOST TOUCHED AND GRATIFIED BY YOUR KIND MESSAGE ALLOWING ME TO INFORM IN-DIA THAT YOU WHO OCCUPY UNIQUE POSITION IN IMAGINATION OF INDIAN YOUTH ARE CON-VINCED THAT DECLARATION OF HIS MAJESTY'S GOVERNMENT SUBSTANTIALLY CONFERS THAT FREEDOM FOR WHICH INDIAN NATIONALISM HAS SO LONG STRUGGLED. (April 1, 1942)

On the heels of this telegram came one from Arthur Moore, editor of the Calcutta daily, *The Statesman*:

Your message to Sir Stafford Cripps inaugurates the new era. Nothing can prevent it. I am glad that my eyes have seen this salvation coming. (April 1, 1942)

By now negotiations had started between Cripps and the Congress leaders.

Arthur Moore the very next day sent to his paper an editorial comment on Sri Aurobindo's message:

We have not doubted that Sir Stafford Cripps' mission will succeed nor were we depressed by Tuesday's wave of pessimism.... But since then an event has happened which will change a whole army of doubters and pessimists into optimists. After listening to Sir Stafford's broadcast, Sri Aurobindo has, from his Ashram in Pondicherry, offered his public adhesion 'in case it can be of any help in your work'. Rarely in history can so great a help have been so unostentatiously offered. This is the release not only upon India but upon the world of a great spiritual force which has long been awaiting its appointed time. (New Delhi, April 2, 1942)

Seeing that the negotiations with the Congress were not going right Sri Aurobindo decided on a further intervention. This took two forms. On the one hand he sent messages to some important figures in Indian politics. Through Mr. Shiva Rao he communicated to Mahatma Gandhi and Pandit Nehru that Cripps's offer should be accepted unconditionally. He also sent a couple of telegrams. One was to Rajagopalachari, Birla House, New Delhi:

IS NOT COMPROMISE DEFENCE QUESTION BET-
TER THAN RUPTURE. SOME IMMEDIATE SETTLE-
MENT URGENT FACE GRAVE PERIL. HAVE SENT
DURAISWAMI INSIST URGENCY. APPEAL TO YOU
TO SAVE INDIA FORMIDABLE DANGER NEW FOR-
EIGN DOMINATION WHEN OLD ON WAY TO SELF-
ELIMINATION. (April 2, 1942, 9-30 a.m.)

The reference to the danger of a new foreign domination was
evidently to the presence of Japanese forces approaching India. The other telegram was addressed to 'Dr. Moonje, Hindu
Mahasabha, New Delhi':

SETTLEMENT INDIA BRITAIN URGENT, FACE AP-
PROACH GRAVE PERIL MENACING FUTURE IN-
DIA. IS THERE NO WAY WHILE RESERVING RIGHT
REPUDIATE RESIST PARTITION MOTHERLAND
TO ACCEPT COOPERATION PURPOSE WAR INDIA
UNION. CANNOT COMBINATION MAHASABHA
CONGRESS NATIONALIST AND ANTI-JINNAH
MUSLIMS DEFEAT LEAGUE IN ELECTIONS BENGAL
PUNJAB SIND. HAVE SENT ADVOCATE DURAISWA-
MI IYER TO MEET YOU. (April 2,1942, 9-30 a.m.)

Here an important point is the great possibility of a division
within the country due to Jinnah's movement to separate
Muslims from Hindus. One of the salutary effect of accepting the Cripps Proposals would be to keep India united in the
face of the Japanese threat and thus lead to an unpartitioned
free India in the future.

As the telegrams indicate, Sri Aurobindo also took the
extraordinary step of sending a personal representative

so that his appeal might go home better to the wrangling negotiators. Nirodbaran in his book *Twelve Years with Sri Aurobindo* has memorably painted the scene:

> …It was the evening hour. Sri Aurobindo was sitting on the edge of his bed just before his daily walking exercise. All of us were present; Duraiswami, the distinguished Madras lawyer and disciple, was selected as the envoy, perhaps because he was a friend of Rajagopalachari…. He was to start for Delhi that very night. He came for Sri Aurobindo's blessings, lay prostrate before him, got up and stood looking at the Master with folded hands and then departed.(…) We may remind ourselves of Talthybius' mission to Troy in Sri Aurobindo's epic poem *Ilion*. (…) Similarly, Duraiswami went with India's soul in his "frail" hands and brought it back, down-hearted, rewarded with ungracious remarks for the gratuitous advice.[1]

Nirodbaran has also written:

> (…) Cripps flew back a disappointed man but with the consolation and gratified recognition that at least one great man had welcomed the idea. When the rejection was announced, Sri Aurobindo said in a quiet tone, "I knew it would fail." We at once pounced on him and asked him, "Why did you then send Duraiswami at all?" "For a bit of *nishkama karma*[2]," was his calm reply, without any bitterness or resentment. The full spirit of the

1. *Twelve Years with Sri Aurobindo*, published by Sri Aurobindo Ashram, Pondicherry, 2010, pp.142-43.
2. Disinterested work, the essence of which is that the work is inwardly dedicated to the Divine with no attachment to the result.

kind of 'disinterested work' he meant comes out in an early letter of his (December, 1933), which refers to his spiritual work: "I am sure of the results of my work. But even if I still saw the chance that it might come to nothing (which is impossible), I would go on unperturbed, because I would still have done to the best of my power the work that I had to do, and what is so done always counts in the economy of the universe." (…) We know the aftermath of the rejection of the Cripps Proposal…: confusion, calamity, partition, blood-bath, etc., and the belated recognition of the colossal blunder.[3]

Gradually the colossal blunder is being rectified in general conformity with, though not yet in precise adherence to, the vision expressed by Sri Aurobindo when on his seventy-fifth birthday on August 15, 1947, India obtained her independence and, as Nirodbaran puts it:

Sri Aurobindo's 'bardic' voice was heard once again", declaring about the partition of British India into India and Pakistan as a price of freedom: "…by whatever means, in whatever way the division must go: unity must and will be achieved for it is necessary for the greatness of India's future.[4]

Nirodbaran has noted that:

Sri Aurobindo's prediction has been half-fulfilled, for

---

3. *Twelve Years with Sri Aurobindo*, published by Sri Aurobindo Ashram, Pondicherry, 2010, Pp.144-45
    4. *Ibid.*, p.145

Bangladesh (East Pakistan) is now entirely independent…[5]

We may conclude our account with a significant letter written by M. C. Desai, on September 29, 1942 to the Bombay daily, *The Times of India*. It is entitled "Complex of Dependency" and runs:

It is amusing to find such Congress and liberal stalwarts as Mr. Rajagopalachari and Sir Chimanlal Setalvad openly advocating almost unconditional acceptance of the Cripps Proposals and denouncing the Congress leaders for rejecting them.

But what the Indian man-in-the-street would like to know is why these wise and eminent gentlemen did not speak out their real mind at the right time when Sir Stafford Cripps was here. What prevented 'C. R.', for instance, from the Congress Working Committee during the negotiations, when he knew it was giving a wrong lead to the country?

Similarly, one remembers that Sir Chimanlal Setalvad saw Sir Stafford Cripps on behalf of the Indian Liberals and submitted their resolution. They elaborate resolution did not fail to emphasise such minor omissions in the scheme as that of a specific mention of women's vote in the provincial plebiscite. But on the crucial question whether the country should accept or reject the scheme the resolution neither definitely said yes or no – quite like the Liberals.

5. *Twelve Years with Sri Aurobindo*, published by Sri Aurobindo Ashram, Pondicherry, 2010, fn on p. 145

Curiously, the solitary Indian statesman who took a realistic view and had the courage of his conviction to advise his countrymen unequivocally to accept the Cripps Proposals was that mystic and visionary of Pondicherry — Shri Aurobindo Ghose. The belated wisdom of our leaders emphasises the truth of the ancient Sanskrit proverb: 'The Brahmin always thinks too late.'

Instead of harping on the Mahatma's admittedly 'unpractical idealism', let our leaders organise a countrywide educative propaganda to convince the wide mass of the people of the wisdom of accepting a compromise solution like the Cripps plan if India's problem is to be resolved peacefully and create opportunities for ordinary people to express their honest opinion."

References

This essay by Amal Kiran [K.D. Sethna] is taken from *Aspects of Sri Aurobindo*, Reprinted by Clear Ray Trust, Pondicherry, 2000, pp. 144-49.

Brahma Drishti and *Brahma Tej*

Sisir Kumar Mitra

The Yoga that Sri Aurobindo started at Baroda and pursued in Calcutta, he perfected at Pondicherry. This perfection meant for him possession and mastery of the spiritual powers of Yoga through which to help forward the evolution of man to a higher status above the mind. To this he devoted himself exclusively. His spiritual power was always active upon world affairs, and when necessary, he publicly intervened and took a direct part. In a certain context he said that he had never had any will which had not been fulfilled.

In one of his early letters — written in 1905 [. . .] Sri Aurobindo said that he had possessed and would use his spiritual force which he called *Brahma tej* to bring about the political liberation of his country, mentioning at the same time that this force is superior to the force of arms *(Kshastra tej).*

The words of admission of King Visvamitra after a total rout of his tremendous military forces at the hands of Rishi Vashistha ring in the ears of a student of India's history: *'Dhigbalam kshatriyabalam brahma tejo balam balam.'* (Fie upon the force of arms, the spiritual force is the force of forces.) With Sri Aurobindo, this belief in it was no mere intellectual belief. With him it was a tested truth. "It was this force which, as soon as he had attained it, he used, at first only in a limited field of personal work, but afterwards in a constant action upon world forces. He had no reason to be dissatisfied with the results or to feel the necessity of any other kind of action."

Sri Aurobindo used his Yogic force on certain world movements. He said:

> In Spain — in Madrid — I was splendidly successful.… In Ireland and Turkey the success was tremendous. In Ireland I have done exactly what I wanted to do in Bengal.[1]

> I was one of the influences that worked to make it (the Russian Revolution) a success.[2]

In the mid-twenties Sri Aurobindo remarked:

> The experience of humanity would have remained incomplete without the experiment in Russia.[3]

Later, he wrote:

> Russia is different — unlike the others it has lingered in medieval religionism and not passed through any period of revolt — so when the revolt came it was naturally anti-religious and atheistic. It is only when this phase is exhausted that Russian mysticism can revive and take not a narrow religious but the spiritual direction.[4]

Now came one of those early-foreseen upheavals in which he was to take part. It was the Second World War. The Truth-vision of both Sri Aurobindo and the Mother discerned in

---

1. Nirodbaran, *Talks with Sri Aurobindo*, p.44.
2. A.B.Purani, *Evening Talks with Sri Aurobindo*, 2007, p. 474.
3. A.B. Purani, *Evening Talks with Sri Aurobindo*, 2007, p. 157
4. Sri Aurobindo, *On Yoga*, Vol.II, pp.200-01.

it an upsurge of the Asuric or anti-divine forces with Hitler
and his satellites as the spearhead of their attack upon the
Allied Powers that stood for the higher values of life. The
joint declaration they made ran as follows:

> We feel that not only is this a battle waged in just self-
> defence and in defence of the nations threatened with the
> world-domination of Germany and the Nazi system of
> life, but that it is a defence of civilisation and its highest
> attained social, cultural and spiritual values and of the
> whole future of humanity. To this cause our support and
> sympathy will be unswerving whatever may happen; we
> look forward to the victory of Britain and, as the eventual
> result, an era of peace and union among the nations, and
> a better and more secure world-order.

Hard was it for such a declaration, so sharply contradictory
to prevailing ideas, to go down with an unbelieving world.
They had therefore to emphasise and re-emphasise this truth
in several other statements clearing up its implications and
people's doubts. In one of these Sri Aurobindo said:

> You should not think of it as a fight for certain nations
> against others or even for India; it is a struggle for an
> ideal that has to establish itself on earth in the life of hu-
> manity, for a Truth that has yet to realise itself fully and
> against a darkness and falsehood that are trying to over-
> whelm the earth and mankind in the immediate future.
> It is the forces behind the battle that have to be seen and
> not this or that superficial circumstance. It is no use con-
> centrating on the defects or mistakes of nations; all have
> defects and commit serious mistakes; but what matters is

on what side they have ranged themselves in the struggle. It is a struggle for the liberty of mankind to develop, for conditions in which men have freedom and room to think and act according to the light in them and grow in the Truth, grow in the Spirit. There cannot be the slightest doubt that if one side wins, there will be an end of all such freedom and hope of light and truth and the work that has to be done will be subjected to conditions which would make it humanly impossible; there will be a reign of falsehood and darkness, a cruel oppression and degradation for most of the human race such as people in this country do not dream of and cannot yet at all realise. If the other side that has declared itself for the free future of humanity triumphs, this terrible danger will have been averted and conditions will have been created in which there will be a chance for the Ideal to grow, for the Divine Work to be done, for the spiritual Truth for which we stand to establish itself on the earth. Those who fight for this cause are fighting for the Divine and against the threatened reign of the Asura.

Behind the Nazi aggression characterised by Sri Aurobindo as 'the peril of black servitude and a revived barbarism threatening India and the world', were those forces of Darkness which were out not only to destroy human civilisation with all its higher values but also to frustrate the Divine Work of Sri Aurobindo and the Mother — the work of liberating man from his bondage to these forces into the freedom and power of a New Light from above that would transform man into his destined divine perfection. When these hostile forces found that their sovereignty over the earth was challenged they attempted, said Sri Aurobindo, an attack on the

Mother's body. But as he concentrated exclusively on repelling it without even allowing a shade of the black force to fall on the Mother, the attack came on him. It was on 23rd November 1938, that is, on the eve of the 24th November Darshan, and about a year before the outbreak of the Second World War, Sri Aurobindo had an impacted fracture of the right thigh — just an external instance of how 'the Warrior of the Ages' gave in his war with the adverse forces, so that the ultimate victory might be his and man grow in his strength to receive the Light the time for whose Manifestation was drawing near. Indeed, the nearer was the Manifestation, the fiercer was the resistance of the hostile forces which, says Nolini Kanta, no earthly power could hit back. Sri Aurobindo's self-abnegation is in line with Shiva the Nilkantha's and Dadhichi's with the same end — saving the world from the asuric hold.

The next occasion that called for his personal intervention was when Britain in seeking India's co-operation in the war effort made an offer to her — one of those which Sri Aurobindo had foreseen and to which he attached great value. The offer was made in March 1942 through Sir Stafford Cripps, a member of the British Cabinet, and an eminent statesman of sincere convictions, whose stand for India's independence free India afterwards fully appreciated.

As in the case of the War, this also was looked upon with the same dubious mind. While the people and leaders of India, save a few, read into it sinister designs of the British to exploit her man-power and other resources during the war and then back out of their promises after the victory, Sri Aurobindo found in it a welcome opportunity for India's advancement, her ultimate political liberation and a step on the way to her self-fulfillment. He had previsioned such a deal.

It was, in his view, a 'real' negotiation between the British Government and the Indian leaders. The occasion impelled his personal intervention. He promptly sent a message to Sir Stafford Cripps in the course of which he said:

> …I welcome it as an opportunity given to India to determine for herself and organise in all liberty of choice her freedom and unity and take an effective place among the world's free nations. I hope that it will be accepted and the right use made of it putting aside all discords and divisions. I hope too that a friendly relation between Britain and India replacing the past struggles will be a step towards a greater world union in which as a free nation her spiritual force will contribute to build for mankind a better and happier life.

He followed it up by sending personal messages to C. Rajagopalachari, one of the leading brains of the Congress High Command, and to B. S. Moonje, leader of the Hindu Mahasabha, and sent S. Duraiswamy Iyer, an eminent advocate of the Madras High Court, and a disciple, as his personal envoy to the Congress Working Committee at Delhi.

The viewpoints which Sri Aurobindo instructed his envoy to place before the Congress leaders, as Duraiswami himself has stated them to the writer, were: (1) Japan's imperialism being young and based on industrial and military power and moving westward, was a greater menace to India than the British imperialism which was old, which the country had learnt to deal with and which was on the way to elimination. (2) It would be better to get into the saddle and not be particular about the legal basis of the power. Once the power came into our hands and we occupied seats of power, we could establish our positions and assert ourselves. (3) The proposed Cabinet would provide opportunities for the Congress and the Muslims to understand each other and pull together for the country's good, especially at that time of the crisis. (4) The Hindu Mahasabha also being represented, the Hindus, as such would have a chance of proving their capacity to govern India not only for the benefit of the Hindus but for the whole country. (5) The main problem was to organise the strength of India in order to repel the threatened aggression.

Sri Aurobindo held that by accepting the Cripps offer India would be able to take part in the administration of the country as also in the war effort as a co-partner with Britain and the solution of Cripps could be turned into a means of India's independence. The Congress took it as an invitation to co-operate but not as an equal partner.

As always, so in the present instance, Sri Aurobindo was for dynamic action in the political field. His idea was that the acceptance of the proposals, though short of the mark, would lead at once to India's industrial and economic improvement and to an efficiently up-to-date military training for her youth — the objectives for which the Congress had been fighting for years. Another important consideration was that it was to the Congress, the largest representative body of the land, that the offer was made. Therefore there could arise no two-nation theory, no division of the country with its deadly and disastrous consequences. Some of the Congress leaders, however, admitted afterwards that the decision of the Congress should have been otherwise.

But the Congress chose to go by their own reasons rather than pay heed to the Seer, one who for the first time after his retirement in 1926 made a public pronouncement on a subject he regarded as of vital consequence to the destiny of his country. The second instance of the tragic failure of the human mind to rise to the truth beyond itself. Truly has the Poet said:

> For man shall not know the coming till its hour
> And belief shall be not till the work is done.[1]

Sri Aurobindo was aware that his advice would not be accepted. Why did he then make the effort, he was asked. — 'I have done a bit of *"nishkama karma"* (disinterested work)', was his smiling reply.

Yet it is a fact that, despite the contrary policy of the Congress, the country gave to the British Government in India large co-operation through which they could raise the strength of the Indian army to a force of two million, the biggest figure in its history, recruit large numbers as technicians, expand and modernise ordnance factories and other industries, and carried the war on to a successful finish with the help of Indians and improved resources. One wonders how free India could stand, how, for instance, she could save Kashmir or Hyderabad, or take a responsible part in international assignments, as in Korea or Indo-China, if she had not a number of capable military leaders, mechanised troops and other sections, seasoned in the last war, to face the situation after the British personnel, at any rate, the major part of it, had left. The Divine works out his purpose even when man fails to understand him.

---

1. Sri Aurobindo, *Savitri*, Bk. I, p.57

Reference

This is an extract from Sisir Kumar Mitra's *The Liberator — Sri Aurobindo, India and the World,* pp.213- 19, published by Jaico, Bombay,1970.

A Sadhak's Account

Then came the famous Cripps Proposals. In the evening Sir Stafford Cripps broadcast his Proposals to the Indian people, from Delhi; they were discussed everywhere. In P's room the radio was installed and a connection made to Sri Aurobindo's room so that he might listen to the war-news and reports from all quarters of the globe, except from the Axis zones.

The next day at about 2 p.m., after the All India Radio news at 1:30, there was a hot discussion among three sadhaks, including P, in his room. P took the stand point of the purely spiritual man who judges by looking at what is behind appearances. It seemed that he had already spoken with the Mother and thus was arguing forcefully for the acceptance of the Proposals. The second person was an experienced politician of the Gandhian Congress days and took the negative position. He argued the pros and cons of the Proposals and was of the opinion that the Indian leaders would reject them. The third coma, a novice, with no political experience, was more for its acceptance. The discussion became hotter and hotter, so much so that the Mother, while going from Her bathroom to Her dressing room, was attracted by the unusual volume of sound. She did not enter Her dressing room, but turned Her steps towards P's room. Before entering there She heard part of the argument. Then She stepped in and asked, "What is it all about?" P said that one person argued that Cripps' offer would not be accepted by the Indian leaders. The Mother felt amused and inquired, "Why?" By then She had sat on the chair that was in front of Her. It was a very unusual and interesting scene; the Mother, still in Her beautiful Japanese kimono just out of the bath didn't seem to care to change Her dress, and was more interested in the arguments against the acceptance. Then she began to talk with a very calm and distinct voice. One could see that She who had entered a few minutes ago had been transported somewhere else and the voice was coming from that plane….

She said something to this effect:

> One should leave the matter of Cripps' offer entirely in the hands of the Divine, with full confidence that the Divine will work everything out. Certainly there were flaws in the offer. Nothing on earth created by man is flawless, because the human mind has a limited capacity. Yet behind this offer there is the Divine Grace directly present. The Grace is now at the door of India, ready to give its help. In the history of a nation such opportunities do not come often. The Grace presents itself at rare moments, after centuries of preparation of that nation. If it is accepted, the nation will survive and get a new birth in the Divine's consciousness. But if it is rejected the Grace will withdraw and then the nation will suffer terribly, calamity will overtake it.
>
> Only some moments ago, the same Grace presented itself at the door of France, immediately after the fall of Dunkirk, in the form of Churchill's offer to her to have joint nationality with England and fight the enemy. Sri Aurobindo said that it was the right idea, and it would also have helped His work immensely. But France could not raise herself above the ordinary mind, and rejected it. So the Grace withdrew and the Soul of France has gone down. One doesn't know when the real France will be up again.

But India with her background of intense spiritual development through the ages, must realise the Grace that is behind this offer. It is not simply a human offering. Of course its form has been given by the human mind, and it has elements of imperfection in it. But that does not matter at all. Have faith in the Grace and leave everything to the Divine who will surely work it out.

My ardent request to India is that she should not reject it. She must not make the same mistake that France has done recently and that has plunged her into the abyss.

As soon as She had finished speaking She hurried back to Her dressing room, without a word or a look at anybody. Later, on the same day, the first of April, 1942, when She returned from the Prosperity after the distribution, She disclosed that Sri Aurobindo had already sent a telegram to Sir Stafford, and the latter had reciprocated very heartily, and both the telegrams were being put on the notice board by Nolini. We then read the messages and were very much encouraged.

But the next day or the day after it the Congress announced that it had rejected the offer. The Mother was quite unperturbed; She only said, "Now calamity will befall India."

The events that followed in India right up to now need no mention. We have been paying all along for our mistake.

Reference

This extract is from *Twelve Years With Sri Aurobindo* by Nirodbaran, published by Sri Aurobindo Ashram, Fourth Edition 2010, pp. 145-48.

The Mother in front of the map of India

The Mother on The Cripps Proposal

Mother, I was asking… (laughter) You said that India was free in 1915, but was she free as she is free now? Because India is not free as one whole. She is broken up.

Oh! Oh! That's what you wanted to know.

That… the details were not there. No, there must have been a possibility of its being otherwise, for, when Sri Aurobindo told them to do a certain thing, sent them his message, he knew very well that it was possible to avoid what happened later. If they had listened to him at that time, there would have been no division. Consequently, the division was not decreed, it was human deformation. It is beyond question a human deformation.

But then, how can it be said that the decision of the Supreme cannot be eluded?

What?

If the Divine had chosen that India would be free…

No, no, it's not like that, my child! (*Laughter*)
It's a *fact*, that's all. It is the Divine who is India, it is the Divine who is freedom, it is the Divine who is subjection, it is the Divine who is everything – then how could He choose?

(*silence*)

I advise you to go up there and see, then you will understand. So long as you have not climbed right up the ladder, it
will be difficult to understand.

18th January 1956

(*Questions and Answers 1956*, CWM 2nd Ed., CWM, Vol.8, pp. 31-32)

*

Sweet Mother,

*Why did Sri Aurobindo advise India's leaders to accept
the Cripps Proposal in 1942, when he knew fully well that
they would not?*

*The Divine often advises or tries to guide man, know-
ing very well that His help will be refused. Why then does
He do it?*

The Divine *always* informs, but it is rare indeed for men to
listen to Him. Either they do not hear Him or do not believe
Him.

Men always complain of not being helped, but the truth
is that they refuse the help which is *always* with them.

5th May 1965

(*Some Answers from the Mother – I*, CMW 2nd Ed.,
Vol. 16, p. 318)

*

It was the repetition of the same stupidity as when Cripps
came to make his proposal, when Sri Aurobindo sent a message saying, "Accept, whatever the conditions, otherwise it

will be worse later on." That's what Sri Aurobindo told them. Gandhi was there and he retorted, "Why is this man meddling? He should be concerned only with spiritual life."

(A conversation of 17th November 1962)

THE POINT OF VIEW OF THE
INDIAN LEADERS

Jawarharlal Nehru with Sir Stafford Cripps

Nehru and His Stand

Sunayana Panda

For the youth of today's India it will not be easy to imagine the place of high respect and honour that was given to Jawaharlal Nehru during his lifetime. The freedom struggle was a movement that took on, almost from the beginning, a spiritual turn and people looked up to those who were in this movement as men and women worthy of their hearts' worship.

Ironically, most of those who spearheaded the freedom struggle had been educated at some point or the other in Britain — starting with Sri Aurobindo and Subhas Chandra Bose to Mahatma Gandhi, Jawaharlal Nehru, Sardar Patel and Mohammad Ali Jinnah. They understood what was being denied to the Indians. They had seen the British in their own country and witnessed how trade and commerce, culture and education flourished in a free country.

Nehru had been educated in Harrow and in Cambridge, in educational institutions which set the standards of excellence. But when he came back to India and began his career as a lawyer he realised that this was not going to be the main activity of his life. Very soon he turned to the Freedom Movement.

Our impressions of Nehru come from the photographs which we see of him. He appears before us as sophisticated, immaculately dressed and westernised. We tend to think that he lived a life of comfort and ease. In fact, he spent more than 3000 days of his life behind bars. Fareed Zakaria, the noted journalist wrote:

In all Nehru spent 3262 days during the prime of his life in various jails. He was jailed for the first time in December 1921and for the last time he came out of the prison was in January 1945. In other words from the age of 32 to the age of 56 he spent the major part of his life behind bars — a sacrifice rarely seen in the history of human freedom.

Hidden behind the large outlines of history are the little untold tales of personal loss and hardship. While he was moved from one prison to another, at a time when he readily accepted to undergo this form of isolation, his father passed away and there was no one to look after his mother, his wife and his daughter. During one of his imprisonments his mother had a stroke, his wife was diagnosed to be suffering from tuberculosis and his daughter was sent away to boarding school. In spite of this Nehru remained determined not to give up.

In order to get a glimpse into the mind and heart of Nehru it is enough to read what he said in court to the British judge when he was being tried in Gorakhpur before being imprisoned in 1942. These were his touching words: "I stand before you, Sir, as an individual being tried for certain offences against the state. You are a symbol of that State. But I am also something more than an individual — I too am a symbol of Indian nationalism, resolved to break away from the British Empire and achieve the independence of India."

It is easy for us to say that the leaders could not see the importance of the proposal brought by Cripps. The fact is, we have the advantage of looking at the story several decades after it happened, and in hindsight everything can be explained so easily. We can see things which were not so obvious to those who were living these events, those who sat through the discussions and were trying to read between the lines.

When Sir Stafford Cripps came with this famous proposal there was a general feeling of hope and it was a step which was appreciated by the members of the Congress. According to R. Coupland, the only person who was unhappy about the visit was Jinnah. Coupland was a professor of Colonial History at University of Oxford, who at the time of Cripps' visit was asked by him to join his staff and so he had a close view of the events.

Nehru arrived in Delhi after Cripps had been there and had started his talks with the other leaders. Those who don't know Nehru's life may wonder why he was not there already. The fact is he was in Allahabad for the wedding of his daughter, Indira. How momentous an occasion it was is difficult to understand for people who are not familiar with Indian life or Indian history. Indira was Nehru's only child and had grown up without her father's presence in her life. While he languished in jails Nehru was worried that he could not be with his daughter, that he could not guide her or protect her. He kept in touch with her through letters and even tried to pass on his knowledge to her through these letters.

Nehru could not have left such an important duty — of giving away his daughter in marriage — to come to the negotiating table. But it is a sign of his greatness that he left Allahabad the very next day to reach Delhi and get informed about the talks that had already taken place.

Since this visit by Cripps was connected to the Second World War it is important to know something about how this war was perceived by the Indians. This world war had come at a time when in India some people had already been fighting their own battles against British Imperialism for a long time. For the freedom fighters this became suddenly an opportunity to find a common enemy and the leaders as well as the common man in India began to imagine that by joining hands with Hitler they would carry on the same war that they had been fighting against the British but with greater help. There was a great deal of goodwill among Indians for Nazis in Germany as they were seen as those who would defeat the British and bring them to their knees.

It was a time when India was just waking up to an awareness to international issues. Much of the country still lived at the rhythm of the feudal societies which had been established for centuries in the subcontinent and the majority of people did not even understand the issues which were at stake. The sense of geography was still at a very basic level. Those who were literate could better understand what was going on because news of the war came through the daily papers and the radio. To the youth of India of the twenty-first century this must be hard to understand. Everyone is now so used to seeing the news round the clock, presented by various channels and every little thing being analysed by experts.

The war created even greater difficulties of governance. The country lived in extreme poverty and the war was going to make it difficult to procure basic necessities. Already the burden of being occupied by a foreign power was weighing on the minds of the leaders, now there would also be the problems that all countries face during a war.

Gandhi opposed the Second World War on grounds of non-violence. The whole of India opposed the war efforts because they thought that the Nazis were going to defeat the British and in this way end the British Empire. They imagined this would automatically bring freedom to India. Indians went so far as wishing the defeat of the Allied Forces. The psychology was, "the enemy of my enemy is my friend."

When the Second World War was declared Mahatma Gandhi started an anti-war campaign. Following his wishes Nehru also spoke at large gatherings, urging people not to support the war. Here is a portion of a speech he gave:

> I am convinced that the large majority of the people of England are weary of empire and hunger for a real new order. But we have to deal not with them but with their Government and we have no doubt in our minds as to what that Government aims at. With that we have nothing in common and we shall resist it to the uttermost. We have therefore decided to be no party to this imposed war and to declare this to the world. This war has led already to widespread destruction and will lead to even greater horror and misery. That is why we must dissociate ourselves from this war and advise our people to do likewise and not help in anyway with money or men. That is our bounden duty.

It seems strange that even educated men could not see the danger that the Nazis represented.

The point at which Sir Stafford Cripps was sent to India, there was a real threat that the Japanese would invade India. And this made the whole proposal so urgent. However, those who were going to participate in the discussions were thinking more of the future and of where the Hindus and the Muslims would stand after the British had left.

Nehru writes in his book *Discovery of India* about his reaction when he first saw the proposal. This is what he says:

> I remember that when I read those proposals for the first

time I was profoundly depressed, and that depression was largely due to the fact that I had expected something more substantial from Sir Stafford Cripps' proposals as well as from the critical situation that had arisen. The more I read those proposals and considered their many implications, the greater was my feeling of depression. I could understand a person unacquainted with Indian affairs imagining they went far to meet our demand. But, when analysed, there were so many limitations, and the very acceptance of the principle of self-determination was fettered and circumscribed in such a way as to imperil our future.

According to Nehru, the main obstacle to the proposal came from the fact that the British wanted to give the option of not joining the Indian Union to any state that did not want to join it. This could mean in theory that the country could be divided into not two but many pieces. Jinnah was adamant about getting Pakistan for the Muslims but the others did not want the country to break up. Although it is generally believed that the British wanted to "divide and rule" from what Churchill and Cripps themselves say this was not really on their agenda. But giving the choice to any state that wanted to remain independent it opened the doors to many theories.

Once again Nehru's book *The Discovery of India* gives us an insight of what went on in the minds of the Congress leaders.

Any proposal to cut up India into parts was a painful one to contemplate; it went against all those deeply-felt sentiments and convictions that move people so powerfully. The whole nationalist movement of India had been based on India's unity, but the sentiment was older and deeper than the present phase of nationalism; it went far back into the remote periods of Indian history. That belief and sentiment had been strengthened by modern developments till it had become an article of faith for vast numbers of people, something that could not be challenged or controverted. A challenge had come from the Moslem League but few took it seriously, and there were certainly large numbers of Moslems who did not agree with it. Even the basis of that challenge was not really territorial, though it suggested a vague undefined partition of territory. The basis was a medieval conception of nations based on religious differences, and according to it, therefore, in every village in India there were two or more nations. Even a partition of India could not get over these widespread and overlapping religious divisions. A partition would in fact add to the difficulty and increase the very problems it was intended to solve.

Apart from sentiment, there were solid reasons against partition. The social and economic problems of India had reached a crisis, chiefly because of the policy of the British Government, which necessitated rapid and all-round progress if the gravest of disasters had to be averted. That progress could only take place with real and effective planning for the whole of India [...]. To think of partitioning India at this stage went against the whole current of modern historical and economic development. It seemed to be fantastic in the extreme.

Coupland gives us the British point of view. This is what he writes in his book:

The purpose of the non-accession provisions was manifest. They embodied the British Government's considered reply to the Moslem claim to Pakistan. It was unfair
to say, as Hindu critics promptly said, that they directly
encouraged the partition of India. On the contrary, they
pointed the way by which alone (in the present writer's
view) partition can be avoided. For they are based on a
profound psychological truth. The story of the forbidden
fruit applies to great affairs of life as much as small. The
certain method of whetting a nation's or a community's
appetite for something is to say that it is the one thing
they may not have. Thus, just as there is small chance of
India wanting to stay in the British Commonwealth unless she is free to go out, so the best hope of a single Indian Union is to assure the people of the predominantly
Moslem areas that they need not join it unless they wish.
As Sir Stafford said in his broadcast, the door must be left
open. [. . .]

We can now see how the ruler and ruled thought with different minds. The words of the proposal were weighed and
reweighed but each side saw the situation from a very different point of view. The British temperament was so different from the Indian one. How did they ever manage to live
together at all for two centuries? Looking back at the whole
story of the British Empire from the twenty-first century all
we can say is that it served the purpose of unifying the country and of bringing India to the modern age. If India is an
economic power today the roots of the success lie somewhere
in the story of colonisation. It was perhaps a price we had to
pay in order to become a nation and a democracy. But what
a heavy price it was!

To get back to Nehru, let us see through his eyes how the Indian leaders of the time weighed the pros and cons. Nehru writes in *The Discovery of India*:

> The decision about the future of the Indian States was not going to be made by the people of those States or their chosen representatives but by their autocratic rulers. Our acceptance of this principle would have been a negation of our well-established and often repeated policy and a betrayal of the people of the States, who would have been condemned to autocratic rule for a much longer period. [...]
>
> No federation can be deemed in the interest of India, if in it representatives of the provinces are compelled to sit with the nominees of irresponsible rulers. There is, in fact, no answer to Mr. Gandhi's claim that the Princes are bound to follow the Crown in its transfer of authority to the people.' Prof. Keith had given this opinion in regard to the earlier proposal of the British Government relating to Federation, but it was even more applicable to the proposals brought by Sir Stafford Cripps.
>
> The more one thought of these proposals the more fantastic they grew. India became a chequer-board containing scores of nominally independent or semi-independent States, many of them relying on Britain for military protection of autocratic rule. There was to be neither political nor economic unity, and Britain might well continue to exercise dominating control, both politically and economically, through the many petty States it controlled.

Rajmohan Gandhi writes in his biography of the Mahatma,

the stand that he took in regard to the proposal brought by Cripps. He writes:

> Invited to New Delhi to meet Cripps, Gandhi could not swallow the balkanisation, nomination by princes, or a class in the scheme that placed India's defence during the war wholly in British hands.

In fact, Gandhi is supposed to have been rather radical in his opposition to the proposal. He is supposed to have said, 'If this is your entire proposal to India, I would advise you to take the next plane home.' He is supposed to have declared that this proposal was like a postdated cheque on a failing bank.

The suggestion that the Indian army would be command-ed by British generals was one more reason why the Congress was unwilling to accept the proposal. From the biography written by Peter Clarke it would seem that in the end it was this which tipped the balance and what was a certain victory for Cripps on the eve of the final announcement turned out to be a total failure. Of course, no one can say today what was discussed in the final meeting after which this proposal was totally rejected.

We now live in a world which is wired together and know that after all is said and done people of all countries and races are essentially one. Although the horrors of the partition are far behind us and the younger generation is quite ignorant about the details of that phase of our history, there is a very good reason even today to reflect on the need for giving up the hatred that existed in the past and to live as one large family. It is not any more important to think about why it happened, it is more important to try and know the past so that we do not sit and make judgments on anyone, to look at others with more compassion.

Jawaharlal Nehru visited the Ashram twice and each time he was given a very warm reception. He came to Pondicherry in connection with the independence of Pondicherry from French rule. We remain grateful to him for allowing the French to continue to run their educational and cultural institutions in Pondicherry. When he passed away the Mother gave a very moving message:

> Nehru leaves his body but his soul is one with the Soul of India that lives for Eternity.

We can not end this chapter without quoting what Jawaharlal Nehru wrote about Sri Aurobindo so that we remember that he held the Master in high regard. In his foreword to Dr. Karan Singh's book *Prophet of Indian Nationalism* Nehru wrote the following words:

> It is extraordinary that a person who spent fourteen of the most formative years of his life, from the age of 7 to 21, cut off from India and steeped in the European classics and the England of his day, should have become, in later years, the brilliant champion of Indian nationalism, based on the philosophic and spiritual background of Indian thought. His whole career in active politics was a very brief one, from 1905 to 1910 when he retired to Pondicherry...During these five years he shone like a brilliant meteor and created a powerful impression on the youth of India.

This is what Sri Aurobindo wrote about Nehru:

But peace? Peace is never easy to get in the life of the world and never constant, unless one lives deep within and bears the external activities as only a surface front of our being. And the work he has to do is the least peaceful of all. If Buddha had to lead the Indian National Congress, well! For the spiritual life there is perhaps no immediate possibility: his mind stands in between, for it has seized strongly the Socialist dream of social perfection by *outward* change as the thing to be striven for and has made that into a sort of religion. The best possible on earth has been made by his mind its credo: the something beyond he does not believe in, the something more here would seem to him a dream without basis, I suppose. But pray for him, of course, he is a man with a strong psychic element and in this life or another that must go beyond the mind to find its source.

I have not read Jawaharlal's book and know nothing of his life except what is public; now of course I have no time for reading. But he bears on himself the stamp of a very fine character, a nature of the highest sattwic kind, full of rectitude and a high sense of honour, a man of the finest Brahmin type with what is best in European education added — that is the impression he gives. I must say that Mother was struck by his photograph when she first saw it in the papers, singling it out from the mass of ordinary *eminent* people.[1]

---

1. *Letters on Himself and the Ashram,* Vol.35, The Complete Works of Sri Aurobindo, p.193.

Sir Stafford Cripps with Gandhi

Gandhi's Comments

Gandhi wrote in his paper *Harijan* on April 19th 1942:

> It is a thousand pities that the British Government should have sent a proposal for dissolving the political deadlock, which on the face of it, was too ridiculous to find acceptance anywhere and it was a misfortune that the bearer should have been Sir Stafford Cripps, acclaimed as a radical among radicals and a friend of India.

He also stated:

> I have no doubt about his (Sir Stafford's) good-will. He believed that no one could have brought anything better for India. But he should have known that at least the Congress would not look at Dominion Status even though it carried the right of secession. The very moment it was taken he knew too that proposal contemplated the splitting up of India into three parts, each having difference ideas of governance. It contemplated Pakistan, and yet not the Pakistan of the Muslim League's conception, and last of all it gave no real control over Defence to responsible Ministers.
>
> The fact is that Sir Stafford Cripps, having become part of the Imperial machinery, unconsciously partook of its quality. Such is its strength. It is the almost the invariable experience in India that those Indians who are drawn into it lose their originality and become like their companions in the service and often outdo the latter in their

loyalty to the moloch of Imperialism. Had Sir Stafford remained detached, he would have conferred with his radical friends in India and secured their approbation before undertaking his very difficult mission. If it be said in answer that he could not very well do so, that is exactly what I mean when I say that, having become part of the machinery, he was bound to fall under its spell and could not do the obvious thing.

But it is no use brooding over the past of British mistakes. It is more profitable to look within. The British will take care of themselves if we will take care of ourselves. Our mistakes or rather defects are many. Why blame the British for our limitations? Attainment of independence is an impossibility till we have solved the communal tangle. We may not blind ourselves to the naked facts. How to tackle the problem is another question. We will never tackle it so long as either or both parties think that independence will or can come without any solution of the tangle. There are two ways of solving what has almost become insoluble. The one is the royal way of non-violence, and the other of violence. In the first way the formal consent or co-operation of the other party is unnecessary. If there is a dispute between two ways over the ownership of an apple, the non-violent way is to leave the apple for the other party to take, the latter well knowing that it would mean non-co-operation on the surrendering party's part.

The second way is the usual way of violence. There the party's fight with each other till one is for the time being worsted. All interested in freedom have to make the choice. I suppose the choice has already been made by the chief actors. But the rank and file do not know their own minds. It is necessary for them, if they can, to think independently, and take to non-violent action in terms of unity.

It consists in Hindus and Muslims on the wayside fraternising with another, if they believe that joint life is a perfect possibility, nay a necessity whether those who believe in the two-nation theory and communal partition of India can live as friends co-operating with one another I do not know.

If the vast majority of Muslims regard themselves as a separate nation having nothing in common with the Hindus and others, no power on earth can compel them to think otherwise, and if they want to partition India on that basis, they must have the partition, unless Hindus want to fight against such a division. So far as I can see such preparation is silently going on on behalf of those parties. That way lies suicide. Each party will want British or foreign aid. In that case goodbye to independence. The fight will then range round not independence but the imaginary apple after the manner of the imaginary days. I did not contemplate the actuality. I should not like to be its living witness. I would love to see a joint fight for independence. In the very process of securing independence it is highly likely that we shall have forgotten our quarrels. But if we have not, it will be then only time to quarrel, if we must.

Reference

The Cripps Mission, edited by Sukhamay Banerjee and Shanti Mitra published by Bamabo, Calcutta 1942, pp 64-66.

Sir Stafford Cripps and C. Rajagopalachari

C. Rajagopalachari Resigns

This was the resolution passed in the Madras Legislature:

The Madras Legislature Congress Party notes with deep regret that the attempts to establish a National Government for India to enable her to face the problems arising out of the present grave situation have failed and that, as a result of this, Nationalist India has been placed in a dilemma. It is impossible for the people to think in terms of neutrality, of passivity during an invasion by an enemy power. Neither is it practicable to organise any effective defence independently and un-co-ordinated with the defence measures of the Government. It is absolutely and urgently necessary in the best interests of the country at this hour of peril to do all that the Congress can possibly do to remove every obstacle in the way of the establishment of a national administration to face the present situation, and, therefore, as much as the Muslim League has insisted on the recognition of the right of separation of certain areas from United India upon the ascertainment of the wishes of the people of such areas as a condition precedent for a united national action at this moment of grave national danger, this party is of opinion and recommends to the All-India Congress Committee that to sacrifice the chances of the formation of a national Government at this grave crisis for the doubtful advantage of maintaining a controversy over the unity of India is a most unwise policy and that it has become necessary to choose the lesser evil and acknowledge the Muslim League's claim for separation; should the same be persisted in when the time comes for framing a constitution for India and thereby remove all doubts and fears in this regard and to invite the Muslim League for a consultation for the purpose of arriving at an agreement and securing the installation of a National Government to meet the present emergency.

*

The Congress party did not take this favourably, and Rajagopalachari had no option but to obey his conscience and resign:

April 30, 1942.

Dear Maulana Saheb,

With reference to your observation on the resolutions passed on my motion by the Madras Congress Legislative Party, I admit that I should have talked the matter over with you and other colleagues of the Working Committee before moving the resolutions, knowing as I did their disagreement on the subject. I write this to express my regret.

I have explained to you already how strongly I feel. I believe that I should be failing in my duty if I do not endeavour to get people to think and act in the direction which my conviction leads to. I feel that in the public interests I should move the resolutions already notified by Mr. Santanam; I desire, therefore, to request you to permit me to resign my place in the Working Committee.

Let me tender my grateful thanks for the unqualified trust and affection bestowed on me by you and the other colleagues during all these many years that I have served in the committee.

Yours sincerely
C. Rajagopalachari

Reference

India Wins Freedom by Abul Kalam Azad, Orient Longmans, Calcutta, 1959, pp. 67 –69

Resolution of the Congress Working Committe

Issued 11th April 1942

The Working Committee have given full and earnest consideration to the proposals made by the British War Cabinet with regard to India and the elucidation of them by Sir Stafford Cripps.

These proposals, which have been made at the very last hour because of the compulsion of events, have to be considered not only in relation to India's demand for independence but more especially, in the present grave war crisis, with a view to meeting effectively the perils and dangers that confront India and envelop the world.

Congress has repeatedly stated, ever since the commencement of the war in September 1939, that the people of India would line themselves with the progressive forces of the world and assume full responsibility to face the new problems and shoulder the new burdens that had arisen, and it asked for the necessary conditions to enable them to do so to be created. The essential condition was the freedom of India, for only the realisation of present freedom could light the flame which would illuminate millions of hearts and move them to action.

At the last meeting of the All-India Congress Committee, after the commencement of the war in the Pacific, it was stated that: "Only a free and independent India can be in a position to undertake the defence of the country on a national basis and be able to help in the furtherance of the larger causes that are emerging from the form of war."

The British War Cabinet's new proposals relate principally to the future, upon the cessation of hostilities. The Committee, while recognising that self-determination for the people of India is accepted in principle in that uncertain future, regret that this is fettered and circumscribed and that certain provisions have been introduced which gravely imperil the development of a free and united national government and the establishment of a democratic state. Even the constitution-making body is so constituted that the people's right of self-determination is vitiated by the introduction of non-representative elements.

The people of India have, as a whole, clearly demanded full independence, and Congress has repeatedly declared that no other status except that of independence for the whole of India could be agreed to or could meet the essential requirements of the present situation.

The Committee recognise that future independence may be implicit in the proposals, but the accompanying provisions and restrictions are such that real freedom may well become an illusion.

The complete ignoring of ninety millions of people in the Indian States, and their treatment as commodities at the disposal of their Rulers, is a negation both of democracy and self-determination. While the representation of an Indian State in the constitution-making body is fixed on a population basis, the people of the State have no voice in choosing those representatives, nor are they to be consulted at any stage while decisions vitally affecting them are being taken. Such States may in many ways become barriers to the growth of Indian freedom, enclaves where foreign authority still prevails, and where the possibility of maintaining foreign-armed forces has been stated to be a likely contingency and a perpetual menace to the freedom of the people of the States as well as of the rest of India.

The acceptance beforehand of the novel principle of non-accession for a Province is also a severe blow to the conception of Indian unity and an apple of discord likely to generate growing trouble in the Provinces, and which may well lead to further difficulties in the way of the Indian States merging themselves into an Indian Union. Congress has been wedded to Indian freedom and unity and any break of that unity especially in the modern world when peoples' minds inevitably think in terms of ever larger federations would be injurious to all concerned and exceedingly painful to contemplate. Nevertheless the Committee cannot think in terms of compelling the people of any territorial unit to remain in an Indian Union against their declared and established will. While recognising this principle, the Committee feel that every effort should be made to create conditions which would help the different units in developing a common and co-operative national life. Acceptance of this principle inevitably involves that no changes should be made which would result in fresh problems being created and compulsion being exercised on other substantial groups within that area. Each territorial unit should have the fullest possible autonomy within the Union consistent with a strong National State.

The proposal now made on the part of the British War Cabinet encourages and will lead to attempts at separation at the very inception of the Union and thus create great friction just when the utmost co-operation and goodwill are most needed. This proposal has been presumably made to meet the communal demand, but it will have other consequences also and lead politically reactionary and obscurantist groups among the different communities to create trouble and divert public attention from the vital issues before the country.

Any proposal concerning the future of India must demand attention and scrutiny, but in to-day's grave crisis it is the present that counts and even the proposals for the future in so far as they affect the present. The Committee necessarily attached the greatest importance to this aspect of the question and on this ultimately depends what advice they should give to those who look to them for guidance. For this the present British War Cabinet's proposals are vague and altogether incomplete, and there would appear to be no vital changes in the present structure contemplated. It has been made clear that the defence of India will in any event remain under British control. At any time Defence is a vital subject; during war-time it is all-important and covers almost every sphere of life and administration. To take away Defence from the sphere of responsibility at this stage is to reduce that responsibility to a farce and nullity, and to make it perfectly clear that India is not going to be free in any way and her Government is not going to function as a free and independent Government during the pendency of the war.

The Committee would repeat that the essential fundamental prerequisite for the assumption of responsibility by the Indian people in the present is their realisation as a fact that they are free and are in charge of maintaining and defending their freedom. What is most wanted is the enthusiastic response of the people, which cannot be evoked without the fullest trust in them and the devolution of responsibility on them in the matter of Defence. It is only thus that even in this grave eleventh hour it may be possible to galvanise the people of India to rise to the height of the occasion. It is manifest that the present Government of India, as well as its Provincial agencies, are lacking in competence and are incapable of shouldering the burden of India's defence. It is only the people of India, through their popular representatives, who may shoulder this burden worthily. But that can only be done by present freedom and full responsibility being cast upon them. The Committee are, therefore, unable to accept the proposals put forward on behalf of the British War Cabinet.

Reference

Transfer of Power 1942-7, Vol.1, Cripps Mission, January - April 1942, edited by Nicholas Mansergh and published by Her Majesty's Stationery Office, London, 1970, reprinted in India by Vikas Publications, Delhi, pp.745 – 48.

THE POINT OF VIEW OF THE BRITISH

The Draft Declaration for Discussion with Indian Leaders

(The conclusions of the British War Cabinet as set out below are those which Sir Stafford Cripps has taken with him for discussion with the Indian Leaders.)

30 March 1942

His Majesty's Government, having considered the anxieties expressed in this country and in India as to the fulfilment of the promises made in regard to the future of India, have decided to lay down in precise and clear terms the steps which they propose shall be taken for the earliest possible realisation of self-government in India. The object is the creation of a new Indian Union which shall constitute a Dominion, associated with the United Kingdom and the other Dominions by a common allegiance to the Crown, but equal to them in every respect, in no way subordinate in any aspect of its domestic or external affairs.

His Majesty's Government therefore make the following declaration:

(a) Immediately upon the cessation of hostilities, steps shall be taken to set up in India, in the manner described hereafter, an elected body charged with the task of framing a new Constitution for India.

(b) Provision shall be made, as set out below, for the participation of the Indian States in the Constitution-making body.

(c) His Majesty's Government undertake to accept and implement forthwith the Constitution so framed subject only to:

(1) the right of any Province of British India that is not prepared to accept the new Constitution to retain its present constitutional position, provision being made for its subsequent accession if it so decides. With such non-acceding Provinces, should they so desire, His Majesty's Government will be prepared to agree upon a new Constitution, giving them the same full status as Indian Union, and arrived at by a procedure analogous to that here laid down.

(2) the signing of a Treaty which shall be negotiated between His Majesty's Government and the constitution-making body. This Treaty will cover all necessary matters arising out of the complete transfer of responsibility from British to Indian hands; it will make provision, in accordance with the undertakings given by His Majesty's Government, for the protection of racial and religious minorities; but will not impose any restriction on the power of the Indian Union to decide in the future its relationship to the other Member States of the British Commonwealth.

Whether or not an Indian State elects to adhere to the Constitution, it will be necessary to negotiate a revision of its Treaty arrangements, so far as this may be required in the new situation.

(d) The constitution-making body shall be composed as follows, unless the leaders of Indian opinion in the principal communities agree upon some other form before the end of hostilities:

Immediately upon the result being known of the provincial elections which will be necessary at the end of hostilities, the entire membership of the Lower Houses of the Provincial Legislatures shall, as a single electoral college, proceed to the election of the constitution-making body by the system of proportional representation. This new body shall be in number about one-tenth of the number of the electoral college.

Indian States shall be invited to appoint representatives in the same proportion to their total population as in the case of the representatives of British India as a whole, and with the same powers as the British Indian members.

(e) During the critical period which now faces India and until the new Constitution can be framed, His Majesty's Government must inevitably bear the responsibility for and retain control and direction of the defence of India as part of their world war effort, but the task of organising to the full the military, moral and material resources of India must be the responsibility of the Government of India with the co-operation of the peoples of India. His Majesty's Government desire and invite the immediate and effective participation of the leaders of the principal sections of the Indian people in the counsels of their country, of the Commonwealth and of the United Nations. Thus they will be enabled to give their active and constructive help in the discharge of a task which is vital and essential for the future freedom of India.

Reference

Transfer of Power 1942-7, Vol.1, Cripps Mission, January - April 1942, edited by Nicholas Mansergh and published by Her Majesty's Stationery Office, London, 1970, reprinted in India by Vikas Publications, Delhi, pp. 565-66.

Sir Winston Churchill, Prime Minster of Great Britain

Churchill's Statement in the House of Commons

The crisis in the affairs of India are rising out of the Japanese advance has made Britain wish to rally all the forces of Indian life to guard their land from the menace of the invader. In August 1940 a statement was made about the aims and policy which we are pursuing in India. This amounted in short to a promise that as soon as possible after the war India should attain Dominion Status in full freedom and equality with this country and other Dominions under a constitution to be framed by Indians by agreement amongst themselves and acceptable to the main elements in the Indian national life.

This was, of course, subject to the fulfilment of our obligations for the protection of minorities, including the Depressed Classes and our treaty obligations to the Indian States and a settlement of certain lesser matters arising out of our long association with the fortunes of the Indian Sub-Continent. However, in order to close these general declarations with precision and to convince all classes, races and creeds in India of our sincere resolve the War Cabinet have agreed unitedly upon conclusions for present and future actions which, if accepted by India as a whole, would avoid alternative dangers of either that the resistance of a powerful minority might impose an indefinite veto upon the wishes of the majority or that a majority decision might be taken which would be resisted to a point destructive of internal harmony and fatal to the setting up of a new Constitution.

We had thought of setting forth immediately the terms of this attempt by a constructive contribution to aid India in the realisation of full self-government. We are, however, apprehensive that to make a public announcement at such a moment as this might do more harm than good. We must first assure ourselves that our scheme would win a reasonable and practical measure of acceptance and thus promote concentration of all thought and energies upon the defence of the native soil.

We should ill-serve the common cause if we made a declaration which would be rejected by the essential elements in the Indian world and which would provoke fierce constitutional and communal disputes at a moment when the enemy is at the gates of India.

Accordingly we propose to send a member of the War Cabinet to India to satisfy himself on the spot by personal consultation that the conclusions upon which we are agreed and which we believe represent a just and final solution will achieve their purpose. The Lord Privy Seal and Leader of the House, Sir Stafford Cripps has volunteered to undertake this task. He carries with him the full confidence of His Majesty's Government and he will strive in their name to procure the necessary measure of assent, not only from the Hindu majority but also from those great minorities amongst which the Moslems are most numerous and on many grounds prominent.

The Lord Privy Seal will at the same time consult with the Viceroy and the Commander-in-Chief on the military situation bearing always in mind the paramount responsibility of His Majesty's Government by every means in their power to shield the people of India from the perils which now beset them. We must remember that India has great part to play in the world struggle for freedom and that her helping hand must be extended in loyal comradeship to the valiant Chinese people who have fought alone so long.

We must remember also that India is one of the bases from which the strongest counter blows must be struck at the advance of tyranny and aggression.

Sir Stafford Cripps will set out as soon as convenient and suitable arrangement can be made. He will command in his task heartfelt good wishes of all parts of the House and meanwhile no words will be spoken of debates held here or in India which would add to the burden he has assumed in his mission or lesson the prospects of good result. During Sir Stafford Cripps' absence from Parliament his duties as Leader will be discharged by the Foreign Secretary, Mr. Eden.

Reference

The Cripps Mission edited by Sukhamay Banerjee and Shanti Mitra, published by Bamabo, Calcutta, October 1942, pp. 12-14

Sir Stafford Cripps Arrives

(Sir Stafford Cripps arrived by air at Delhi on March 22. The same afternoon he called a Press Conference, and in the course of his opening address to it he said:)

I have come to India to discuss with the leaders of Indian opinion, conclusions which the War Cabinet have unitedly reached in regard to India. I am here to ascertain whether these conclusions will as we hope be generally acceptable to Indian opinion. Obviously it would not be appropriate for me to say anything further about the precise nature of the proposals at this stage beyond the indications which were given by the Prime Minister in the House of Commons. Their chief object is to set out finally and with precision the practical steps which His Majesty's Government proposed as the method of fulfilling their past promises of self-government to the Indian peoples. We believe that a generally acceptable line of practical action can be laid down now and thus the main obstacle to India's full co-operation in her own defence will have been removed. We feel confident that with the political atmosphere thus clarified the leading political organizations will be enabled to put forward their maximum effort in preserving their country from the brutalities of aggression. How best their effective participation in the councils in their country can be immediately arranged will be another matter for discussion.

I have come here because I am, as I have always been, a great friend and admirer of India and because I want to play my part as a member of the War Cabinet in reaching a final settlement of the political difficulties which have long vexed our relationship. Once these questions are resolved, and I hope they may be quickly and satisfactorily resolved, the Indian peoples will be enabled to associate themselves fully and freely not only with Great Britain and the other Dominions but with our great Allies, Russia, China, and the United States of America so that together we can assert our determination to preserve the liberty of the peoples of the world.

There is no time to lose and no time for long discussions. I am sure in the circumstances of today the leaders of the main parties and interest in India will be ready take quick decisions.

My intention is to stay at Dehli for two weeks, for there are many urgent an important matters to be attended to in England, and I believe that within that time with energy and goodwill the essentials of success be achieved. During so short a visit I shall, of course, not be able to travel about in the country and see everyone I should like to meet. I hope that my friends in India will understand that my time is short and will forgive me if I am unable to see them before I leave.

My association in the past has been more close with my friends in the Congress than with the members of the other parties or communities, but I am fully impressed with the need to any scheme for the future of India to meet the deep anxieties which undoubtedly exist among the Moslems and the other communities. I shall, therefore, embark upon my task equally open to all points of view-Hindu, Moslem, Sikh and others.

I believe that the proposals of the War Cabinet will appeal to the Indian leaders since they are the unanimous results of the deliberations of a body of people over known in the past to have widely differing outlooks upon the Indian question.

I shall be spending the first two days with the Viceroy,

who has cordially welcomed me in and shall then have the opportunity of meeting the Commander-in-Chief and other members of the Executive Council and the Provincial Governors. The Indian National Congress, the Muslim League, the Chamber of Princes and the Hindu Mahasabha have been asked to nominate their own representatives to hold discussions with me and representatives of the Sikhs, the Liberal Party, and the Scheduled castes have also been invited to meet me. I shall of course see other representative people including Provincial Premiers.

I am confident that both the Indian press and the press in other interest countries will give their help in the great cause of Indian self-government and defence and will not by ultimately speculation or by the spreading of uninformed and ill-considered rumours prejudice the chance of a successful settlement of the outstanding issue.

Reference

The Cripps Mission edited by Sukhamay Banerjee and Shanti Mitra, published by Bamabo, Calcutta, October 1942, pp. 17-19.

Winston Churchill during the Second World War

Winston Churchill and His Views

Sunayana Panda

Many young Indians today may not be familiar with the name of Sir Winston Churchill. He is one of those individuals whose name will always be linked to the Second World War and in that context he is seen as a heroic figure who led Britain to Victory during her hour of trial and difficulty. However, in India he has an image which is not so grand. His reluctance to give independence to India is well-known and this is why he appears as a symbol of British Imperialism and a stumbling block in the way of India's progress.

Many tend to think that his perception of India was distorted because he did not know the country and that his impressions were all second-hand and from a distance. This is far from true. Churchill was actually posted in India, more precisely in Bangalore, in his youth. He admitted that he turned to reading and vastly increased his knowledge of the world during that period because life in Bangalore was so boring. Not having gone through a university education, because he joined the army as soon as he could, he never missed an opportunity to catch up by reading, especially about history. Not only his years in Bangalore but also his participation in the war in the North West Frontier Province gave him a very close view of the Indians and their way of life. India, therefore, was not really just an impression.

To Indians his personality may seem quite intriguing. He was someone who had seen action in the battlefields but at the same time he was a writer and had a mastery over ideas and words. And in order to relax his mind and to take a break from his stressful work of running a government he had very unusual hobbies – painting and brick-laying. This must be totally baffling to an Indian mind. How can a Prime Minister, a statesman and writer, actually do such manual work as laying bricks? There are photographs of Churchill where one can see him working shoulder to shoulder with those who were re-doing the roof of his house. He was also a bon vivant, someone who enjoyed his food, wine and cigars. This is totally the opposite of what the typical Indian hero was to the generation that grew up during and soon after independence. Those who fired the imaginations of the masses were the ones who gave up all luxuries, went through hardships and often imprisonment for the sake of the good of others.

Churchill was the quintessential Englishman of the times: loyal to king and country and deeply convinced that the British were only doing their duty of civilizing the world when they were building their empire. He would have gone to any length to keep the British Empire from falling apart. This is why he was not in favour of granting freedom to India but at the same time he was deeply concerned about the security of the Indian people when the World War broke out. In fact, he took great pride in stating that India had been spared the horrors of the war thanks to the efforts of the British. Here are his exact words:

> No great portion of the world population was so effectively protected from the horrors and perils of the World War as were the peoples of Hindustan. They were carried through the struggle on the shoulders of our small Island.[1]

1. *The Second World War*, published by Cassell & Co. Ltd., London 1951, Vol. IV, The Hinge of Fate, p. 181.

He was in many ways the opposite of Sir Stafford Cripps and in the Indian context they held totally opposing views. While Churchill believed that it was "the white man's burden" to bring order and progress to the lesser races of the world Cripps was all for the independence of India. Cripps was closely connected to many others who were of the opinion that India deserved her place among the free nations of the world.

Churchill's remarks, giving us a glimpse of how they were like chalk and cheese, can be seen in the following extract from his biographer William Manchester:

> Among the unhappiest victims of his gibes was Sir Stafford Cripps. Cripps was one of the very few on Labour's side of the house who shared Churchill's contempt for appeasement; he begged the front bench to rearm before Hitler struck. But he was also ascetic, a vegetarian, a man who shunned coffee and tea and quit smoking cigars because he thought the habit vulgar. "My God," said Churchill when told of this. "Cripps has cut his last tie with human civilization." On another, later occasion, Churchill was airborne over the Sahara Desert when his plane had to land for an emergency repair. Winston stretched his legs and gazed in all directions. "Here we are marooned in all these miles of sand – not a blade of grass or a drop of water or a flower," he said. 'How Cripps would have loved it.'[2]

The war brought things to a critical point and it was no more a matter of personal opinion but something to act on. India was, all said and done, the responsibility of the British.

Fortunately Churchill wrote a great deal and we can, even

2. *The Last Lion Alone* by William Manchester- p. 381

today, turn the pages of his books and get to read his own words where he tells us what went through his mind as the bombs fell and tanks rolled out in various parts of the world. His account of the Second World War, published in four volumes, also shows us how he saw this episode of the Cripps Mission.

We must not forget that it was a war which involved the whole world and so while horrors were unleashed in Europe there was another drama unfolding in Asia. The Japanese were advancing westward and once Hong Kong fell it was clear that India was in danger of being attacked. To the British it was a threat to their power even though they were half way across the world. In India, however, the leaders felt that Japan wanted to invade India only because it was seen as attacking British interests. In their minds they blamed the British for having brought this perceived threat to their homeland.

When Singapore too surrendered those in the British government felt that something very concrete had to be done so that India could be brought into the war. Churchill points out,

> Although only a small extremist section in Bengal, led by men such as Subhas Bose, were directly subversive and hoped for an Axis victory, the powerful body of articulate opinion which supported Gandhi ardently believed that India should remain passive and neutral in the world conflict.[3]

Within ten days of the fall of Singapore Churchill formed a

3. *The Second World War*, published by Cassell & Co. Ltd. London 1951, Vol. IV, The Hinge of Fate, p. 182.

group of ministers who had all actually been to India and had first-hand knowledge of the country. They were asked to advise the War Cabinet about the problem of India. By this time, most senior members of the government were of the opinion that an offer of Dominion status should be made to India.

What exactly was meant by "Dominion status"? Here is what we find in the biography of Churchill, *The Last Lion Alone*, written by William Manchester:

> In the House of Commons, the master blueprint governing the imperial future, the statute of Westminster of 1931, decreed that the Mother Country and her dominions were autonomous communities within the British Empire, equal in status, in no way subordinate to each other in any aspect of their domestic or foreign affairs, though united by a common allegiance, to the Crown and freely associated as members of the British Commonwealth of Nations.

In fact, this question of granting Dominion status had already come up before and Churchill had strongly opposed it, paying rather heavily for it afterwards. In his biographer's words:

> After Ramsay McDonald's Labour party won the election of 1929, Winston held the Exchequer post in Tory shadow cabinet, which would return to power when Labour's slim majority disappeared. But before that could happen, he fell again. The issue was of dominion status for India, putting her on a level with Canada, South Africa, Australia and New Zealand. He, like Disraeli, regarded the

British Raj as the brightest jewel in England's imperial crown. He told Parliament that India was "a geographical term. It is no more a united nation than the equator." Facing a stone wall of hostile Tories, Churchill resigned from the shadow government on January 27th, 1931. Less than seven months later, a new government was formed, and in November, what might have been Churchill's place at the Exchequer was filled by Neville Chamberlain. Thrice fallen from grace, (…) Churchill had become a political pariah, out of joint with the times.[4]

Many in India thought that the Dominion status was either just a bait to get Indian soldiers to fight in the war or it was an outright lie and somehow just another name which would eventually be a modified version of the same colonial status that India would come back to once the war was over. However, if only they had looked towards other countries such as Australia, New Zealand, South Africa and Canada to see that they did not have any difficulties in getting this Dominion status. They were for all practical purposes, free countries.

The war brought out the best in Churchill and this time round the question of India's status acquired utmost importance. Telegrams flew back and forth between him and the Viceroy of India. What made any decision so difficult to arrive at was the fact that India was made up of so many diverse religious groups and each one's feelings and opinions had to be kept in mind. The best thing to do was to send someone to India and discuss the matter with all possible parties. This is how it was decided to send Cripps with the draft declaration. A telegram sent by Churchill to the Viceroy of India shows us

---

4. *The Last Lion Alone* by William Manchester.

the thoughts which were passing through his head.

Telegram: Prime Minister to Viceroy of India 10th March 1942

I agree with you that to fling out our declaration without knowing where we are with the Indian parties would be to court what you rightly call a flop, and start an acrimonious controversy at the worst possible moment for everybody. Yesterday, before I was shown your telegram, we decided not to publish any declaration now, but to send a War Cabinet Minister out to see whether it could be put across on the spot, because otherwise what is the use of having all the trouble? Stafford Cripps, with great public spirit, volunteered for this thankless and hazardous task. He will start almost immediately. In spite of all the differences in our [respective] lines of approach, I have entire confidence in his overriding resolve to beat Hitler and Co. at all costs. The announcement of his mission will still febrile agitation, and will give time for the problem to be calmly solved, or alternatively proved to be, for the time being, insoluble.

My own position is that nothing matters except the successful and unflinching defence of India as a part of the general victory, and this is also the conviction of Sir Stafford Cripps.[5]

Further, it was clear what the intentions behind this propo-

5. *The Second World War*, published by Cassell & Co. Ltd. London 1951, Vol. IV, The Hinge of Fate, p. 190.

sal were. As Churchill says in his book on the Second World War,

> The essence of the British proposal was that the British Government undertook solemnly to grant full independence to India if demanded by a Constituent Assembly after the war.[6]

Whatever might have been the suspicion in the minds of the Indian leaders at least we see here what was there in the minds of the members of the British Government.

In those days communications were not as easy as they are today. Most of the messages that were exchanged were in the form of telegrams. They were quick and they were put down in writing. This made it possible to keep a record of all that was said. Even though Cripps was at the other end of the world, he was in touch on a daily basis with the government back in Britain.

After long negotiations, and after almost coming close to accepting the proposal, the Indian leaders finally decided to decline this offer. On 11th April, Stafford Cripps sent a telegram to Winston Churchill announcing to him the result of all his efforts. Here is a brief excerpt:

Telegram of Lord Privy Seal (Delhi) to Prime Minister

11th April 1942

> I have to-night received long letter from Congress President stating Congress is unable to accept proposals.

6. *Ibid* p. 191.

Rejection on widest grounds and not solely on Defence issue… There is clearly no hope of agreement, and I shall start home on Sunday.

He sent another telegram the same day. Cripps must have felt the need to send a second telegram to clarify the situation as he felt that Churchill might have got news from other sources which were giving him information that had to be explained from his point of view.

> You will have heard of refusal of Congress upon what is almost a new point. But difficulties cannot be explained by telegram.
>
> …We have done our best under the circumstances that exist here, and I do not think you need worry about my visit having worsened the situation from the point of view of morale or public feeling… My own view is that despite failure the atmosphere has improved quite definitely.
>
> …The real difficulty has been the internal feelings in Congress itself; hence their long discussions and the veering of indications of their decisions.
>
> …We are not depressed, though sad at the result. Now we must get on with the job of defending India. I will tell you as to this on my return. All good wishes. Cheerio.[7]

The greatness of Churchill is visible to us in the answer he sent to comfort Stafford Cripps at such a difficult moment in his life. His magnanimity is admirable because on the

7. *The Second World War*, published by Cassell & Co. Ltd. London 1951, Vol. IV, The Hinge of Fate, p. 192

political arena they were rivals. This is how he expresses that moment in his book:

> In the intensity of struggle for life from day to day, and with four hundred million helpless people to defend from the horrors of Japanese conquest, I was able to bear this news, which I had thought probable from the beginning, with philosophy.

He instantly sent a telegram to Cripps to reassure him.

Telegram of Prime Minister to Lord Privy Seal

11th April 1942

> You have done everything in human power, and your tenacity, perseverance, and resourcefulness have proved how great was the British desire to reach a settlement. You must not feel unduly discouraged or disappointed by the result…Even though your hopes have not been fulfilled, you have rendered a very important service to the common cause, and the foundations have been laid for the future progress of the peoples of India.[8]

The war brought the attention of the United States on India and the American President started discussing the matter of India's political status with Churchill in December 1941. Churchill felt that the Americans had "strong opinions and

---

8. *The Second World War*, published by Cassell & Co. Ltd. London 1951, Vol. IV, The Hinge of Fate, p. 185.

little experience" and he did not at all appreciate the way the Americans were trying to advise him on this matter. He says,

> Before Pearl Harbour India had been regarded as a lamentable example of British Imperialism, but as an exclusive British responsibility. Now that the Japanese were advancing towards its frontiers the United States Government began to express views and offer counsel on Indian affairs. In countries where there is only one race broad and lofty views are taken of the colour question. Similarly, States which have no overseas colonies or possessions are capable of rising to moods of great elevation and detachment about the affairs of those who have.[9]

The subject was taken up for discussion once again in February 1942, as it was part of the general planning strategies for the war. Around the time when Cripps was being sent to India Churchill sent a telegram to President Roosevelt:

Former Naval Person to President Roosevelt

4th March 1942

> We are earnestly considering whether a declaration of Dominion status after the war, carrying with it, if desired, the right to secede, should be made at this critical juncture. We must not on any account break with the Moslems, who represent a hundred million people, and the main army elements on which we must rely for the

9. *Ibid.*

immediate fighting. We have also to consider our duty towards thirty to forty million Untouchables, and our treatise with the Princes' states of India, perhaps eighty millions. Naturally we do not want to throw India into chaos on the eve of invasion.[10]

When the talks between Cripps and the Indian leaders failed, President Roosevelt who had been constantly in touch with the British government regarding the developments in India sent a telegram to give the point of view of the Americans on this subject:

President of the United States to Churchill

12th April 1942

> Here the general impression is quite the contrary. The feeling is held almost universally that the deadlock has been due to the British Government's unwillingness to concede the right of self-government to the Indians not withstanding the willingness of the Indians to entrust to the competent British authorities technical, military and naval defence control.
>
> …Should the current negotiations be allowed to collapse because of the issues as presented to the people of America, and should India subsequently be invaded successfully by Japan, with attendant serious defeats of a military or naval character for our side, it would be hard to overestimate the prejudicial reaction on American public

10. *The Second World War*, published by Cassell & Co. Ltd. London 1951, Vol. IV, The Hinge of Fate, pp. 185-186

opinion. Would it not be possible therefore for you to have Cripps's departure postponed on the ground that you personally transmitted instructions to him to make a final effort to find a common ground of understanding? According to my reading, an agreement appeared very near last Thursday night. If you could authorise him to say that he was personally empowered by you to resume negotiations as at that point, with the understanding that both sides would make minor concessions, it appears to me that an agreement might yet be found.[11]

It is sometimes astonishing to see how people whose minds worked in totally different ways were trying to decide the fate of a country about whose culture they knew so little. The President of the United States and the Prime Minister of Great Britain were discussing the future of India, but these two men did not have the same perspective on this question. In fact, Churchill thought that Roosevelt had very little understanding of the situation. This is what he writes about Roosevelt's reflections:

The President's mind was back in the American War of Independence, and he thought of the Indian problem in terms of the thirteen colonies fighting George III at the end of the eighteenth century. I, on the other hand, was responsible for preserving the peace and safety of the Indian continent, sheltering nearly a fifth of the population of the globe. Our resources were slender and strained to the full. Our armies had surrendered or were recoiling

11. *The Second World War*, published by Cassell & Co. Ltd. London 1951, Vol. IV, The Hinge of Fate, p. 193

before the devastating strokes of Japan. Our Navy had been driven out of the Bay of Bengal, and indeed out of most of the Indian Ocean. We had apparently been outmatched in the air. Still, there was the hope and the chance that all could be repaired and that we should not fail in our duty to preserve from hideous and violent destruction the vast, ancient Indian society over which we had presided for nearly two hundred years.[12]

The American President was quite disappointed at the outcome of the talks between Sir Stafford and the Indian leaders. So much so that he asked Churchill to request Cripps to postpone his return and make one more effort to try and convince the Indians to change the decision.

Of course, by then Sir Stafford Cripps was already on his way back home. On 12th April as he flew back from India, Churchill sent a telegram to America which only reveals to us that finally the two Heads of States were only human beings. Even though they did not entirely agree on all decisions Churchill maintained his respect and friendship on a very human level. He had the wisdom not to take a stance that would in any way jeopardize the British and American alliance, knowing that they needed each other to win the World War. This is evident as we can see it in an extract from his telegram to the American President:

Anything like a serious difference between you and me would break my heart, and would surely deeply injure both our countries at the height of this terrible struggle.[13]

12. *The Second World War*, published by Cassell & Co. Ltd. London 1951, Vol. IV, The Hinge of Fate, p. 194

13. *Ibid* p. 195

Looking back at this episode in world history one under-
stands how a few human beings were responsible for the way
India finally faced her destiny.

The spirit of the times brought forth a certain way of
thinking and this coloured all decisions. It is also interesting
to note how the same story told by different people sounds so
different in each version and how we often perpetuate mis-
understandings in each retelling.

Sir Stafford Cripps returned from India but the drama of
the World War continued. Churchill ends the chapter on the
Cripps Mission by writing about how the majority of Indians
continued to think on lines that were so different from his
own and who could not see in how grave a danger they were.
He quotes Gandhi's sentences published in his newspaper on
May 10th:

> The Presence of the British in India is an invitation to Ja-
> pan to invade India. Their withdrawal would remove the
> bait. Assume however that it does not, Free India would
> be better able to cope with invasion...

The extraordinary thing about these two famous figures —
Churchill and Cripps — is that in spite of their being rivals in
the political field they had a mutual respect and understanding for each other. In September 1942 there came a point
in their difference of opinion when Cripps was considering
resigning from the government. Churchill was well aware
that if Cripps did resign then it would have brought about a
situation which would have been "injurious to public interest", as he himself puts it. In the end Cripps decided not to
resign because he did not want to jeopardise the country's
position.

Here is an extract from his letter to Churchill:

> …You have not convinced me that the changes which I have suggested in the central direction of the war are unnecessary. I firmly believe that alterations of that nature are essential if we are to make the most of our war potential.
>
> Such a conviction would have led me to ask you to place my resignation in the hands of H. M. the King, were it not for the special circumstances to which you and my other colleagues have drawn my attention.
>
> I fully realise however, as you have impressed upon me, that this precise moment is one of great anxiety for the country and for the Government. In such circumstances it is clear that nothing avoidable should be done during these particular critical days by the suggestion or disunity or of differences as to the central direction of the war, which might disturb the morale of our fighting men or increase our international difficulties…

It is indeed touching to see how politicians of that era were ready to put aside their personal differences for the sake of the greater good of the country. These were men of a high moral stature, something which we do not find in our times among politicians. Churchill asked Cripps to take charge of the Ministry of Aircraft Production and states his appreciation in his book on the Second World War. He writes,

> I am glad to be able to acknowledge my sense of obligation to him for the loyal and efficient service which he rendered as a Production Minister during those three difficult years.

Although they were such prominent figures of Great Britain of the Second World War years their interactions and their influence on each other remain, sadly, unknown by the common man.

The London Press Comments

The announcement that the Government had decided to send Sir Stafford Cripps to India was given great prominence in the newspapers.

The *Evening Standard* in an editorial thereon said,

> Sir Stafford Cripps has undertaken a mission to India to convince her leaders of the sincere desire of the British people to see India united and free. What precise powers he is given and what exactly is 'just final solution' propounded by the Prime Minister is not known. It is not an easy task to convince India that her problems are to be settled and Sir Stafford is the brave man to do it. He starts with the advantage of long personal friendship with many of India's most beloved leaders. The whole of Britain and the whole free world wishes him well in his difficult undertaking.

The *Evening News* in an editorial entitled a 'Momentous Mission' said

> Mr. Churchill's announcement is a dramatic stroke. Both Sir Stafford and Indians themselves will be working against time. The Japanese will not wait on the conferences on prolonged bargaining.
>
> Unless the spirit of India rises to the heights of the hour, unless quarrels between creeds can be set aside in a common determination to face the common foe, unless Britain is recognised as India's true friend, India may go the way of Singapore, Java and Burma.

Indians standing together with the free peoples can be a bulwark against the tide of savagery from the East. The fate of Hongkong is the fate of Indians and Britons alike if we fail or falter.

Reference

The Cripps Mission edited by Sukhamay Banerjee and Shanti Mitra, published by Bamabo, Calcutta, October 1942, p.15

A Letter from Isobel Cripps

(*For Sri Aurobindo's Centenary, Sri Aurobindo Research Academy brought out a book* Sri Aurobindo — A Garland of Tributes, *edited by Arabinda Basu. Sir Stafford Cripps' wife was asked to contribute to the book. This is her reply.*)

Dear Arabinda,

I am glad to know that you are editing a volume of tributes and essays on the occasion of the Birth Centenary of Sri Aurobindo. I feel honoured and gratified by your invitation to contribute a short description of the background of the formation of and the work of the British Parliamentary Mission led by my late husband Sir Stafford Cripps. I wish so much I could be helpful but I cannot do what you ask. It is 19 years since I was in close contact with the India scene, and though this makes no difference to the warmth of my feelings, there is nothing definite I could write about it all. This is one reason, another is that a definite biography of my husband is about to be written and all material of value has been closed till the biographer decides what he wants.

However I may say that Stafford was very much heartened by Sri Aurobindo's unequivocal message to him. He was especially touched by the fact that Sri Aurobindo offered his public adhesion to the proposals of the Parliamentary Mission and that his message was given wide publicity:

[. . .]

Some of the most eminent political leaders of India subsequently admitted the folly of rejecting the proposals of the British Parliamentary Mission. But I am not surprised that the unerring vision of a spiritual mystic of Sri Aurobindo's stature saw the reality of the situation and that he recommended strongly the acceptance of the proposals.

With all my thoughts and wishes,

Isobel (Cripps)

Muhammad Ali Jinnah with Sir Stafford Cripps

India Misses An Opportunity

Sir Stafford Cripps

(At a press conference in New Delhi on April 11, Sir Stafford Cripps announced that His Majesty's Government's offer to India had been withdrawn.

He said that nothing further could have been done by way of giving responsibility for Defence services to Indian members without jeopardising the immediate defence of India.

In the course of a broadcast from All-India Radio, he said:)

You will have heard that the draft declaration which I brought to India on behalf of the War Cabinet, and which I explained to you last time I spoke over the wireless, has been rejected by your leaders.

I am sad that this great opportunity of rallying India for her defence and her freedom has been missed.

None could have been more fully conscious than I of the great difficulties which history has placed in the way of a settlement of the relations between British and Indian peoples and even more between the different communities in India.

The War Cabinet in sending me upon this mission realised to the full that Indian opinion — though united in the desire for full self-government was widely disunited as to the methods by which it should be attained.

It was with these wide differences of view that we had to deal, and it would have been of no use if we had closed our eyes to the hard realities of the situation.

In the past British Governments have been accused of using vague terms to cloak a lack of purpose; and when they have stated that it must be left to the Indian communities to agree amongst themselves it has been said that this was only a device by which Great Britain might indefinitely retain its control over India.

But Congress has since the outbreak of war repeatedly demanded two essentials as the basis for its support of the Allied effort in the war. First a declaration of Indian independence and second, a Constituent Assembly to frame a new and free constitution for India. Both these demands find their place in the draft declaration.

It was in the light of the demands and criticism of the Indian leaders that the War Cabinet drafted their declaration with the object of convincing the Indian peoples and world public opinion of the sincerity of their desire to offer freedom to India at the earliest practicable moment.

To avoid the complaints that had been made in the past, they put out a clear and precise plan which would avoid all possibility of Indian self-government being held up by the views of some large section or community, but they left it open for the Indian leaders to agree upon an alternative method if they wished.

Of course every individual and organisation would have liked the draft declaration to express his or their point of view, forgetting that if it did, it would inevitably have been rejected by others.

The War Cabinet were thus in a position rather like that of an arbitrator who tries to arrange a fair compromise between conflicting points of view.

They could not, however, without denying the very freedom which they were offering, impose a form of Government upon the Indian peoples which they did not themselves freely choose.

Criticism has been showered on the scheme from all sides; parties and individuals have vied with one another in a competition to discover the greatest number of defects. But in all this spate of criticism, those vital parts of the document with which all agree have never been mentioned. Full and free self-government for India that is its central feature.

This critical and unconstructive attitude, natural enough in the law courts or in the market place, is not the best way of arriving at a compromise, but compromise there must be if a strong and free India is to come into being.

Some day, somehow the great communities and parties of India will have to agree upon the method of framing their new constitution. I regret profoundly for the sake of India, for whom I have a deep and admiring friendship, that the opportunity now offered has not been accepted.

But all this concerns the future. The immediate difficulties have been as regards the present. First there was the difficulty as to defence.

Upon that the attitude of the British Government was very simple. For many decades the defence of India has been in the charge of His Majesty's Government. That charge has been carried out for over twenty years by a Commander-in-Chief who was also Defence Member of the Viceroy's Executive Council.

This has led to an organisation which places the control of the armed forces under a Defence Secretariat containing British and Indian [members], headed by a Commander-in-Chief. The Army units — the Navy and the Air Force all come under this supreme command.

The demand has been made that the defence of India

should be placed in Indian hands. No one suggests that the Commander-in-Chief, as the head of the armed forces, should be under the Indian Government, but they say, his function as defence member should be transferred to an Indian.

This may sound simple — in fact it would mean a long and difficult reorganisation of the whole Defence Secretariat and unscrambling of eggs scrambled many years ago — which would cause delay and confusion at the very moment when the enemy is at the gates and the maximum of speed and efficiency is essential in defence. The duty of the British Government to defend India and our duty to our American allies who are giving such valuable help, makes such a course impossible.

To show our complete sincerity of desire to give to representative Indian members of the Executive the maximum of power, we offered to create a new War Department which would take over the Governmental relations of the Commander-in-Chief's General Headquarters and Naval and Air Headquarters and which would be in his charge as War Member, leaving the rest of the Defence Department — with a number of most important functions added to an Indian Defence Member.

This arrangement satisfied some of the parties but not Congress, who demanded a degree of control in the Indian Defence Member which might have gravely jeopardised the Allied war effort in India.

In the wider area of defence, which touches almost every department of the Government of India, the administration would have been wholly under the control of representative Indians.

But none of these things were the real cause of the breakdown of the negotiations.

In their final letter addressed to me, the Congress Working Committee have stated that the temporary form of Government envisaged during the war, is not such as to enable them to join the government.

They have two suggestions to remedy the situation. First, an immediate change of the Constitution, a point raised at the last moment, and one that everyone else has admitted to be wholly impracticable while the war is proceeding: and second, that they are prepared to enter a true National Government with a cabinet of Indian leaders untrammelled by any control by the Viceroy or the British Government.

Realise what this means the Government of India for an indefinite period by a set of persons nominated by the Indian parties, responsible to no legislatures or electorate, incapable of being changed and the majority of whom would be in a position to dominate large minorities.

It is to understand that the great minorities in India would never accept such a system. Nor could His Majesty's Government, who have given pledges to those minorities, consent to their being placed unprotected while the existing constitution lasts, under a simple and possibly inimical majority rule. It would be a breach to all the pledges that we have given.

Such a solution may sound simple and attractive to those who have no knowledge of the deep communal division in India, but it is in fact wholly impracticable and would never be accepted by very large sections of the Indian peoples.

Congress have suggested that without these changes they cannot give a lead to the Indian people.

The essential need in India to-day is for all the leaders of all the main parties and communities to come together in a single National Government. A scheme that attracts some and repels others, such as Congress has suggested is of little value.

Nor does the precise form matter so greatly. Inspiration and leadership are not to be found in forms or conventions, they will be demonstrated by combined purpose and unity of action.

No constitution and no convention will work unless those who lead the people will come together with a common determination to make it work. Had Congress leaders felt themselves able to join with the other leaders who were willing then indeed a great work might have been accomplished.

One thing I must make clear. I alone in India carry the responsibility for what has been done, neither the Viceroy nor the Commander-in-Chief carries any responsibility for these negotiations. They have throughout done their utmost to help me and I express to them and many other willing helpers of all nationalities my most sincere thanks for that help.

We have tried by the offer that I brought to help India along her road to victory and to freedom, but for the moment, past distrust has proved too strong to allow of present agreement.

But in that failure to achieve immediate results there is no bitterness. Our effort has been genuine. No responsible Indian has questioned the sincerity of our main purpose — the complete freedom of India.

Such an effort inspired by goodwill and sincerity, will leave-its mark upon the history of our relations, and will cast its beneficent light forward into the future. It will prove to have been a first step along the path of freedom for India and of friendship between our two countries.

[...]

Our philosophies, our religions and our traditions differ widely. But in whatever form we may each worship our own conception of supreme power and absolute goodness, we one and all desire to see those ethical and moral standards which are implicit in our religion become the touch stone of our behaviour in all the wide and human constants which make up for day-to-day life.

And in this epic struggle for decent moral standards in the world we fight against the godless barbarism and bestiality of our enemies, but we do not fight alone. Russia, China, the United States of America, and all the allied nations with their suffering peoples, stand beside us, a great company of gallant men and women who will give their all for those things which they know to be right and just. On the battlefields of Russia and China, in their cities and on their farms, millions of our fellow men and women have already given their lives that we might live. To that great and gallant army of the heroic dead we not only owe a debt of gratitude, but we acknowledge a duty and an obligation.

"To strive, to seek, to find and not to yield." To strive, to seek, to find that righteous victory which they died to win, and not to yield to that barbarous aggression against which they made their bodies a living wall of resistance.

It is true that millions have died in those countries, as others have died in the crowded streets of our English cities, in our ships upon the high seas and fighting in our armies on the land and in the air, but as each has fallen others have crowded forward to take the vacant place and countless millions are even now preparing to strengthen and reinforce the effort, to make victory sure.

The hour has struck when India herself is being driven

inexorably by the aggression of Japan into the front line of defence in a war which now spreads its evil tentacles into nearly every country in the world.

India takes her place, and takes it proudly, beside the peoples of Russia, China and America as yet another vast continental area attacked by an unscrupulous and self-seeking foe.

We shall do our utmost, despite all our heavy commitments elsewhere, and the United States of America will lend her great and growing aid as well, to assist the Indians, in the defence of their country. We ask them to help us as we seek to help them. Together we can do much, divided we can do far less.

Hard and difficult times surely lie ahead, the path of honour and of duty has never been an easy one, and today in those who would follow it to its end there must be found a greater courage and determination than ever before; but the end is certain as the slow wheels of justice grind out defeat for the aggressor nations. The vast resources of manufacture of the United States, of Great Britain and of Russia, matched to the unlimited man-power of the Allied nations can bring out one result — the final victory, even though it be delayed, and that towards that victory India can and must play her part, a part that will give her a proud right of full and free representation in the council of the nations when they meet to make the final peace which can, if we will it, lead the peoples of the world into a brighter and happier future of organised and co-operative freedom. As during all wars the tempo of historical development must be acccelerated, so during this the greatest of all wars the speed of advance and the pressure of events will be greater than ever before. The common peoples of the world will have opportunities in the world resettlement such as they have never had before, and the Indian peoples and their leaders   must   make ready to play their full part in the building of the New World Order.

Let us then put aside the discussions of the last month and let them take their ordered place in history, while we turn all our energies to the defence of India, the first step to building a new and free future for the Indian peoples.

This is the time when the youth of the world are called upon to make every sacrifice, to the ultimate sacrifice of life itself, but through that selfless service to humanity they earn the right to take their full share in the shaping of the future. That future must inevitably be influenced by what is done during these anxious days and months of war. Though old heads may be wiser, old hearts cannot have the fire and courage of youth — it is that fire and courage which we must summon to defence of India and to the building of her freedom. When Victory is won risks must be taken, innovations must be tried and we must climb quickly out of the ruts of peacetime habits and customs. A new tempo is needed, a new devotion, a more total effort to finish quickly with the horrors of war and reach that new and constructive era of our world civilisation, upon which we all must concentrate our every energy, once the war is won.

I have seen that effort being made in the Soviet Union, — the whole-hearted devotion of an entire continent — more varied in racial origin than India itself — and the world has learnt — what a great and courageous people inspired with the love of their country and of their freedom can achieve. I have witnessed too the Chinese — ill-equipped — lacking many essential supplies — indomitably carrying on their defence year after year and wearing down the aggressor who has penetrated deep into their homeland. The cities and towns of England have been deeply scarred and her people have suffered as none ever before from the concentrated hate of enemy bombing. Their courage and fortitude have thrilled the world.

Now is the time for India and her peoples to join their courage, their strength and their endurance in this great heroic and world-wide army of the common people, and to take her part in those smashing blows for victory against brutality and aggression which shall for ever free the masses from the age-long fear and tragedy of poverty and of war.

Reference

The Cripps Mission edited by Sukhamay Banerjee and Shanti Mitra, published by Bamabo, Calcutta, October 1942, pp.56-64.